Supervising Counselors
and Therapists

Cal D. Stoltenberg
Ursula Delworth

Supervising Counselors and Therapists

A Developmental Approach

Jossey-Bass Publishers

San Francisco • London • 1987

SUPERVISING COUNSELORS AND THERAPISTS
A Developmental Approach
   by Cal D. Stoltenberg and Ursula Delworth

Copyright © 1987 by: Jossey-Bass Inc., Publishers
                      433 California Street
                      San Francisco, California 94104
                              &
                      Jossey-Bass Limited
                      28 Banner Street
                      London EC1Y 8QE

Library of Congress Cataloging-in-Publication Data

Stoltenberg, Cal D.
   Supervising counselors and therapists.

   (The Jossey-Bass social and behavioral science series)
   Bibliography: p.
   Includes index.
   1. Counselors—Supervision of. 2. Psychotherapists—
Supervision of. I. Delworth, Ursula. II. Title.
III. Series.
BF637.C6S774   1987   158'.3   87-45415
ISBN 1-55542-066-4 (alk. paper)

Manufactured in the United States of America

The paper in this book meets the guidelines for
permanence and durability of the Committee on
Production Guidelines for Book Longevity of the
Council on Library Resources.

JACKET DESIGN BY WILLI BAUM

FIRST EDITION

Code 8737

The Jossey-Bass
Social and Behavioral Science Series

Contents

Contents

 Preface

The supervision of counselors and psychotherapists plays a central role in human service professions and provides a major focus for academic training programs. The belief that "supervision must be viewed as a developmental process" (Sansbury, 1982, p. 53) is shared by many of us who are involved in conducting and researching clinical supervision. Recently, interest in using developmental models to guide practice and research has flourished. But, although an impressive number of journal articles and professional papers have focused on this approach to training, no book has yet attempted to present this model and to explicate its value for practitioners and researchers. *Supervising Counselors and Therapists* will present and review some of the most influential developmental models of clinical supervision and will then propose a complex integration of developmental theory and the supervisory process.

We have spent much of the past decade attempting to understand how the supervisory process operates. Through practice, research, and model building, the central idea of supervision as a developmental process has emerged and guided our work. Developmental models, most of them articulated during the last five years, offer a rich and, we believe, viable route to understanding the process, relationship, and task that we call supervision.

In *Supervising Counselors and Therapists,* we present theoretical constructs from general theories of development to provide a framework within which to examine the supervisory process. Early models of supervision are briefly discussed to set the stage for the emergence of recent developmental approaches. We review seven of these recent approaches and discuss their strengths and limitations. Then we delineate our new, integrated model, highlighting the levels of counselor development and the important supervisory concerns, including assessment, development of supervisors, training environment considerations, and legal and ethical issues.

This material will prove useful to a diverse group of practitioners and scholars in human service areas. Many of our ideas and examples are drawn from the field we know best—psychology and counseling—but we believe these ideas are relevant for allied disciplines such as counseling and guidance, social work, psychiatry, family relations, and pastoral counseling. In addition, private practitioners who supervise unlicensed practitioners or who have a professional interest in the topic will find the book useful. Most important, our students report that knowing something of the model, especially the characteristics of each level and the various settings in which training may occur, is both useful and anxiety-reducing as they progress through the training process. The material may thus be helpful as a primary or secondary text for academic courses and other educational enterprises in which supervision is studied.

Overview of the Contents

In Chapter One, we explore both mechanistic and organismic theories of human development. Although these theories cannot be directly applied to supervision, they nonetheless form the basis of our approach, and serve as a yardstick by which to evaluate our work.

In Chapter Two, we delineate selected theories and models of supervision, with a primary focus on developmental approaches. The model we advocate views supervisee development as a three-level process with an additional level reflecting a high degree of integration across areas of professional practice. We trace the progress of trainees in terms of changes in three structures across eight domains, and we describe supervisory environments specific to each level. An overview of our model is presented in Chapter Three.

In Chapter Four, we explore the first developmental level in which the trainee is dependent on the supervisor yet highly motivated to succeed. Chapter Five describes the second developmental level: The trainee has now gained some experience and has worked successfully with some clients. Trainees at this stage are striving for independence from their supervisors and are more capable of empathizing with and understanding their clients. The third level is outlined in Chapter Six. Trainees at this stage of development usually experience stability of motivation and a reasonable degree of autonomy and are accepting of both themselves and their clients.

Proper assessment of a trainee's developmental level is necessary in order for the supervisor to provide the appropriate supervisory environment to encourage growth. Current assessment procedures, as well as further challenges for the practitioner and researcher, are presented in Chapter Seven. By focusing on the supervisory dyad, we sometimes neglect the total context in which supervision is practiced. In Chapter Eight, we explore various settings and their impact on supervision. A specific model for considering the effects of various training settings is introduced.

The training and development of supervisors, the match between supervisor and supervisee, and the additional approaches of group and peer supervision are examined in Chapter Nine. In Chapter Ten, we examine ethical and legal issues raised by our developmental model. The possible impact of issues of gender and ethnicity, although mentioned in other chapters, is more fully discussed here. Finally, we share some visions of what the practice and study of supervision may become over the next few years and discuss the directions in which developmental models and research may proceed.

At the end of the book we have included some resources to aid the practitioner and researcher in assessing supervision. Resource A offers instruments for assessing supervisors and trainees, Resource B is a trainee information form, and Resource C provides guidelines for conceptualizing a case.

Clinical supervision is an important facet of the training of all mental health professionals. Having a comprehensive model to guide this process is critical if this training is to attain its desired goals. We hope that the model presented in this book will effectively serve this purpose.

Acknowledgments

Writing this book together has provided us an opportunity to renew and expand our colleagueship and friendship, for which we are grateful. For the BRAMJUPS model of supervisor-in-settings, we thank Robert Hoover, Randy Ross, Anita Wollison, Michele Greiner, Joachim Alves-Ferreira, Paul Holt, and Sharon Griffin-Pierson. For skill, patience, and good humor "beyond the call of duty," we thank secretaries Reta Litton, Virginia Travis, and Maggie Ryan. Additional thanks are extended to Brian McNeill and Kim Faulkner for their reviews of earlier drafts of various chapters and for their assistance as "sounding boards" for our ideas. Special thanks to Peggy Stoltenberg for keeping Braden and Ilea under control while we worked on the book.

We are particularly grateful to supervisors who helped us see the meaning in and joy of effective psychotherapy—Saul Toobert, Marvin Moore, Carol Loganbill, and Louise Douce, among others.

A special thank you goes to Karen Pirnot, whose deep and rich understanding of supervisee development gave rise to both the art of her poems and her gift of them to us.

Most of all, we are grateful to supervisees, past and present, who taught us what we did not yet know, challenged us to be all that we could, and in truth are largely responsible for whatever effectiveness we have as supervisors, and for the developmental model we propose.

August 1987   Cal D. Stoltenberg
                                               Norman, Oklahoma

                                               Ursula Delworth
                                               Iowa City, Iowa

The Authors

Cal D. Stoltenberg is an associate professor and director of clinical training for the Counseling Psychology Program in the Department of Educational Psychology at the University of Oklahoma. He was previously a faculty member in the Department of Psychology at Texas Tech University.

Stoltenberg received his B.A. degree (1975) in chemistry and natural sciences from Midland Lutheran College, Fremont, Nebraska, and his M.A. degree (1977) in counseling from the University of Nebraska, Lincoln. He received his Ph.D. degree (1981) in counseling psychology from the University of Iowa. Stoltenberg belongs to numerous professional associations and has been active in psychological organizations at the regional and national levels.

Stoltenberg published his original model of supervision, "Approaching Supervision from a Developmental Perspective: The Counselor Complexity Model," in 1981 while still a graduate student. He has written and edited more than thirty empirical and scholarly publications, including *Social Perception in Clinical and Counseling Psychology* (1984) and *Social Processes in Clinical and Counseling Psychology* (1987).

Ursula Delworth is professor of psychological and quantitative foundations (Counseling Psychology Program) at the University of Iowa. She was previously director of the University Counseling Service there and has also been affiliated with the Western Interstate Commission for Higher Education and Colorado State University.

Delworth received both her B.A. degree in education (1956) and her M.A. degree in counseling from California State University. Her Ph.D. degree in counseling psychology (1969) was awarded by the University of Oregon. Active in a number of professional organizations, Delworth is a former president of Division 17 (Counseling) of the American Psychological Association and has been a member of several groups within this association, including the Education and Training Board and the Committee on Women in Psychology. She is a current member of the Committee on Graduate Education.

Delworth is the author of more than forty publications, including two books: *Crisis Center/Hot Line: A Guidebook to Beginning and Operating* (1972), and *Student Services: A Handbook for the Profession* (1980). Her monograph on supervision, *Supervision: A Conceptual Model* (with C. Loganbill and E. Hardy), was published in 1982. For her scholarly work, Delworth received the Contribution to Knowledge award of the American College Personnel Association and was awarded fellowship status in the American Psychological Association. She is a diplomate in counseling psychology with the American Board of Professional Psychology.

Supervising Counselors
and Therapists

THE FIRST SUPERVISION

My mind is an earthmover.
It scoops up the contents
Of the universal theoretic masterminds.
But I lack knowledge of the architectural terrain.
    So you direct the placement
    Of the contents
    Of my mind.

My mind is both a puzzle and a puzzlement.
My visions allow the totality of the picture,
Yet the fitting of the pieces
Brings frustration and disillusionment.
    So you construct the perimeter of the puzzle
    And encourage me to explore
    The placement of the innermost pieces.

My mind has the makings of a symphony.
But I am unskilled in the writing of the score.
When I attempt the process
It yields an outcome of cacaphony.
    So you rehearse me
    In the playing of the scales
    So that a single melody may emerge.

My mind is pain and pleasure.
It teases me with promise and excitement
And then seeks revenge upon itself
With incompetence.
    So you help me understand that incompetence
    Is simply competence
    Which is yet to be learned, and earned.

When my mind can place its contents in the plan,
And seeks to find harmony from dissonance;
When my mind dares test the creativity of its own music,
And learns the interface of pain with pleasure
    Then your first supervision
    Is finished.
    And mind has begun.

Karen A. Pirnot
University of Iowa

1

Theories of Human Development:

Basis for Understanding the Process of Professional Growth

I recall the first client she ever worked with. She was so anxious and uncertain. Had I not known better, I would have guessed incorrectly who was the client and who was the counselor.

She has developed exceptional skills regarding empathy. It's fascinating to watch her enter into the client's world, the way she seems to feel what the client feels, think what the client thinks. Now, if she could only figure out what to do next.

Sometimes I feel like a spectator. She has come so far, performs so well, knows so much. There doesn't seem to be much I can give to her anymore except a willing ear, a supportive stance, and enthusiastic cheerleading.

—Reflections of a supervisor

We want to consider the process of becoming a counselor or psychotherapist from a developmental perspective, which requires some background in developmental theories. This chapter

introduces the relevant terminology and constructs of development and the systems used to classify developmental theories.
The different world views and basic assumptions of the primary
models will be expanded to discuss the consequences of these
views in terms of their utility for practice and research. The
chapter closes with a discussion of the usefulness of the developmental metaphor as a model for the training of counselors
and psychotherapists.

What Is Development?

"As a primitive, man could never do more than linger at
the threshold of the energy that flickered in his campfire, nor
could he hurt himself beyond Pluto's realm of frost" (Eiseley,
1970, p. 62). With the written word, mankind moved beyond
preoccupation with nature into serious consideration of the
meaning of life and human development. This topic has provided
a focus for philosophers, theologians, scientists, and the common person alike. Framed by historical realities and nurtured
by personal truths, each age has formulated some explicit or
implicit theory regarding the manner and meaning of development. Darwin's evolutionary theses propelled the movement
forward and centered the study of development on nature, on
individuals, and on their interactions. The past one hundred
years have thus been a period rich with thinking and research on
human development.

It is useful to begin with a definition of development.
Baltes, Reese, and Nesselroade (1977, p. 4) provide us with a
starting point by asserting that "developmental psychology
deals with the description, explanation, and modification (opti-
mization) of intraindividual change in behavior across the life
span, and with interindividual differences (and similarities) in
intraindividual change." This definition demands diverse capa-
bilities for a theory of development. It must first be sufficient
to describe behavior changes across time and across individuals
and must then go on to explain why these changes occur in the
order in which they are observed. Finally, the theory should
provide a framework for devising mechanisms to encourage this

process of change. Baltes, Reese, and Nesselroade (1977) note that both the individual's past and present are important in considering the course of development since the focus should be on change and on the processes leading up to specific outcomes.

Salkind (1985) has proposed dimensions to be used in examining theories of development. These include the relative contributions of heredity and the environment, maturation and learning, age, presence or absence of critical periods, continuity or discontinuity of development, and structural considerations (the role of stages and their functions). In addition, he provides criteria for evaluating the usefulness of developmental theories, including inclusiveness, consistency, accuracy, relevancy, fruitfulness, and simplicity. The ideal theory, then, would be consistently applicable to a wide range of human behavior and would accurately predict behaviors relevant to a particular domain of interest. Such a theory should also be parsimonious, remaining as simple as possible while maintaining explanatory and predictive power, and should stimulate and guide research and practice.

These guidelines provide a rigorous set of criteria for use in examining basic assumptions and world views of developmental theories. Before we begin this process, however, a short discussion of how we view scientific theories is in order.

We agree with Baltes, Reese, and Nesselroade (1977), who argue that facts and laws are not present in the natural environment waiting to be discovered. Rather, they are "abstractions imposed on nature by the observer" (p. 17). Theories, then, serve as representations of certain features of the real world—representations subject to interpretation by the scientist and practitioner and necessarily somewhat arbitrary. Therefore, theories cannot be right or wrong, but only more or less useful. Our search then is not for the "correct" theory but for ones that prove most useful in helping us understand and predict our world.

There is another characteristic of theories important for our discussion. Adherence to one particular theory can make it difficult to comprehend other perceptions of reality. Different theories entail different sets of assumptions, which then influence the way we understand and interpret observations (Kuhn, 1962). Not only are theories social creations rather than discoveries, but they can also make it difficult for us to understand other views of the world.

Given this view of scientific theories, how can we begin to make sense of the many developmental theories that exist? Our approach is that there are two important and very different world views—with attendant metaphors and assumptions—that characterize developmental theories. The underlying, divergent metaphors of these two views are the machine and the organism.

The mechanistic approach uses the machine as its basic metaphor. As Baltes, Reese, and Nesselroade (1977) note, this view conceptualizes human development as comparable to discrete parts that operate in a space-time field. This results in an additive model of humans where the whole is equal to the sum of the parts. Change or movement is not a function of goal-oriented behavior but is rather a result of causal forces or antecedent-consequent relationships that can be expressed quantitatively via functional equations. This constitutes a reactive model of human behavior that disallows the role of free will, although the possibility remains that the individual can still believe in free will. The purpose of behavior is derived from its antecedents, resulting in a deterministic view of humans. This view is characteristic of stimulus-response behaviorism, which describes development in purely quantitative terms. This view does not preclude, however, complex combinations of behavioral antecedents utilizing functioning sequences of certain parts or events. That is, a historical perspective that requires certain parts of the person to activate before other parts can function is possible.

The organicism view uses the organism as its basic metaphor for human development. Theories deriving from this model adhere to epistemological constructivism, or an active-organism model where knowledge or reality is constructed by the individual. Importance is not placed on events or combinations of events as much as on the transformation of these events into meaningful information, which is then incorporated into prior knowledge. The developing person is viewed as emerging and moving towards a goal or end state. Behavior is not viewed in deterministic terms but is seen as a function of qualitative differences in structure and form among individuals at various points in development. Quantitative representations of development are made difficult by these qualitative aspects, as well as by the possibility of incidental or chance causes of behavior. In contrast to the mechanistic view of the whole equaling the sum of the parts, the whole is viewed as consisting of more than the sum of the parts. In this model, the whole logically precedes the existence of the parts.

These models can be more simply described as poles or anchors from which to view developmental theories that have been proposed to account for human behavior in various domains. Locke's notion of the infant entering the world as a blank tablet (tabula rasa) upon which experience inscribes ideas and knowledge is characteristic of the mechanistic view. In this perspective, complex ideas are formed from combinations of simple elements, much like an automobile consists of a complex combination of parts performing relatively simple functions or a computer carrying out sophisticated functions through a series of yes-no commands. Piaget (1971) represents the organicism perspective because he believes that experience does not explain everything. There is a contribution to experience provided by the organism that serves to organize and interpret events into increasingly more complex and qualitatively (in addition to quantitatively) different structures.

A number of developmental psychologists have suggested that new models of human development should combine, or at least reflect, features of both the mechanistic and organismic views (for examples, Baltes, 1973; Looft, 1973; Riegel, 1976). It may be necessary to construct discontinuous models for specific domains of development characterized by different age spans or areas that target specific functioning (Baltes, Reese, and Nesselroade, 1977). On the other hand, some investigators support the value of continuity-oriented approaches that apply existing models of development for distinct age groups and domains of functioning to other targets. In the final analysis, the utility of the theory will determine the extent of its application and the amount of research stimulated to test its constructs.

Developmental Theories: Promises and Problems

The theories we examine in this section, although not explicitly concerned with the supervision of psychotherapy, are cognitive-developmental theories that have been influential in providing frameworks for examining more general psychological and cognitive development. The primary focus will be on general concepts relevant to theories of development that emphasize issues crucial in constructing theories applicable to processes usefully viewed as developmental, including counselor training.

Dewey (1938) was instrumental in highlighting the effects of the environment on human development. His notion of progressivism was a cognitive-developmental psychology that viewed person-environment interactions as critically important. Thus, development in the individual could either be enhanced or retarded by the interaction of the organism with the environment. This interactional approach is characteristic of certain currently influential theories of human cognitive development.

For example, Miller (1977) has delineated the basic assumptions of cognitive-developmental theories. He notes that the concept of qualitatively different stages of development can be used to explain growth. Each of these stages, then, builds upon the preceding stages, progressing to an increasingly complex structure. The adaptability of the individual to various environmental demands is a function of the complexity of the structures present at each stage, with increasingly complex and adaptive responses available at higher stages of development. These structures are viewed as stable and irreversible but are subject to influence over time with the appropriate psychological interventions. In reference to the last point, Loevinger (1977, p. 23) has noted that change is only possible because these mental structures are "a bit loose and inconsistent." She refers to an amoeboid movement of personality development and cites Perry's (1968) description of developmental progress as beginning with some insight that goes beyond one's current stage of cognitive development. This bit of insight becomes an "island" of higher-level functioning within a lower stage. This gradually expands until the new structures become predominant and one is functioning largely within a higher stage of development. Piaget (1971) describes this process as a state of equilibrium becoming a state of disequilibrium through a recognition of conflict or inconsistencies between ideas or structures, with subsequent equilibration through insight at a higher level. Perry's (1968) description indicates a gradual expansion of this process across one stage, resulting in a person's movement to a higher stage of development.

Kuhn (1978) reflects the tenets of the organicism model in her discussion of the general assumptions of stage theories. She notes that these theories assume that elements are organized into structured wholes, which are more than merely the sum of the parts. A qualitative reorganization or restructuring occurs at each stage of development, and these stages are constructed by the individual through self-directed actions. Bruner (1964) focuses on the mechanisms for encouraging development by citing the need to specify those experiences that will predispose one to learn, organizing knowledge so that it can be grasped more easily by the individual, and specifying how material can best be presented to facilitate learning. Rest (1973) expands upon these notions by encouraging educators to consider how an individual analyzes and interprets information in making decisions. He also notes that the individual's developmental stage should be considered when sequencing material so that more simple concepts can be learned before more complex material is presented. Finally, he suggests that interaction between the learner and the environment be encouraged so that conditions are favorable for the restructuring of experience.

Piaget's (1971) theory of cognitive development has provided a framework and impetus for much theoretical and empirical work in other domains, such as Kohlberg's (1968) theory of moral development and Loevinger's (1976) discussion of ego development. Piaget (1971) has delineated certain criteria for stage theories. He notes that each stage should be characterized by a general consistency that should be related to structural stages identified in other areas of development. There should be a gradual and sequential upward movement occurring naturally as a result of assimilation (developing in response to internal processes) and accommodation (responding to environmental events). There should also be resistance to regressing to earlier lower stages. These stages should be common among all people from birth through adulthood, and movement through the stages should be facilitated by exposure to certain environments.

Gibbs (1977) has discussed some of the important assumptions of Piaget's model that reflect principles of the organicism model. A key assumption of holism refers directly to analogous structures or organizations at the cellular, neurophysiological, and behavioral levels of functioning that reflect the notion of the sum being greater than its parts. In a similar vein, Gibbs notes the importance of the constructivism assumption that human intelligence extends organic or biological processes. In short, our mental functioning cannot be reduced to its organic makeup. This is partially a function of the interaction of the organism with the environment, which allows for the acquisition of knowledge. The naturalism assumption posits a continuity between humans and other species. This is the "ontogeny recapitulates phylogeny" notion of development that defines a biological basis for the construct of consecutive stages in development. Gibbs (1977) has used this delineation of the components of Piaget's theory to criticize Kohlberg's theory of moral development. The premise of his criticism is that related theories should reflect all of these constructs to adequately fit the model and constitute real stage theories.

Other theorists have pointed to certain problems with stage theories. Loevinger (1977) warns that specific stages of ego development may not be defined by specific behaviors. Harvey, Hunt, and Schroder (1961) caution against equating behaviors with developmental stages. They point out that specific behaviors can be learned without any substantial modification of the structural features of the concept; stages may be only loosely related to particular behaviors. The structural or abstract nature of the concepts is what is important. Recall that one of Salkind's (1985) dimensions for classifying developmental theories was the role of age as a general marker of development. Loevinger (1977) notes that one should not define the characteristics of stages of ego development in terms of age of the individual. Age may be a general benchmark but is at best a crude estimate of development. These conceptual abstractions, then, do not come naturally at certain ages but are produced in interaction with the environment. In contrast to some authors discussed thus far, Loevinger is not convinced that moral or ego development should be hurried. Perhaps all that should be done is to remove the roadblocks to human development to ensure that people are not stuck below their potentially highest level of development. Here person variables, in addition to environmental factors, are alluded to as potential limiting factors.

Thus far in this section we have focused primarily on theories that largely assume an organismic view of the world. These theories are not without their critics. Flavell (1977, p. 249) has stated that "the concept of stage will not figure importantly in future scientific work on cognitive growth." At least part of this criticism comes from the difficulty of confirming or disconfirming stage theory empirically (Kuhn, 1978). Similar criticisms have been leveled by Phillips and Kelly (1975). They note that some stage theories rely on temporal sequences of stages without providing any specifics regarding the relations between these levels. Other theories assume that higher stages incorporate the lower stages, and additional theories describe one stage as replacing an earlier stage. In a contention that sounds similar to a mechanistic position, Phillips and Kelly (1975, p. 172) state that "clearly, hierarchical theory need not be developmental." They note that the simple to complex pattern of hierarchies may be more a description of the order in which behaviors occur rather than new entities; that is, simple behaviors occur in sequences and can be arbitrarily combined into complex behaviors. If one defines a "complex" task as consisting of various "simple" tasks, one should not be surprised to find these hierarchies in examining human behavior.

The primary problem that Phillips and Kelly (1975) have

with stage theories concerns their descriptive versus explanatory power. The definition of development we have chosen for our discussion describes the process of theory construction as one of description, explanation, and modification. Phillips and Kelly (1975) contend that the stages in stage theories have been constructed in terms of higher-order tasks incorporating lower-level tasks. They note that these are merely descriptions based on a logically derived premise. Thus, they cannot be confirmed or disconfirmed because, by definition, experimentation is redundant and will only prove the obvious. They contend that such theories are merely descriptive and not explanatory; thus stage theories are not accessible to research and are of limited value. In a similar vein, Bruner (1968) has noted that the value of Piaget's work is its description of processes but that it lacks a psychological description or explanation of the process of growth.

It is not our purpose to resolve these conflicts within developmental psychology. We do, however, agree with Baltes, Reese, and Nesselroade (1977) that the particular world view one adapts regarding human development will affect both the manner in which one perceives human growth and the design of research to investigate the process. Kuhn (1975) says that the function of data in developmental research should be to further elaborate and articulate the conceptual perspective of the investigator. Thus, how individuals are observed and what data are considered important will differ depending on the theory one brings to the situation.

This discussion of developmental theory has been brief and, perhaps, not as inclusive as some readers would desire. Some of the issues presented, however, will be referred to and expanded upon as we discuss the supervision process in detail in later chapters. Of particular relevance to the developmental model of supervision is the concept of stages of growth that build upon previous stages into increasingly complex structures. The counselor's adaptability is stimulated by the complexity of these structures. Growth from stage to stage is characterized by small areas of higher functioning within a given stage, which expands to other areas until functioning is predominantly at the next higher stage of development. Environmental effects in encouraging development are important, and organizing learning from simple to complex concepts is critical. Although the organicism model appears to us most useful for articulating growth from stage to stage, a mechanistic approach proves useful in examining aspects of learning within particular stages. It is also important, we believe, to avoid equating behaviors, age, or amount of psychotherapy experience with stages of development. Although these factors are useful, they remain crude indicators of development. Finally, one must not lose sight of the important moderating effects of person variables (individual differences) in development.

Theorist as Practitioner

Hunt (1978) argues that the theory-to-practice approach to implementation of developmental models is an illusion. His major assumption is that a developmental theory cannot lead to the direct construction of specific programs to enhance development. Theories that are expressed in impersonal principles without respect to specific individuals in specific places at a given time will lack applications in the impure real world. He suggests that a more balanced view would realize that practitioners are also psychologists (or theorists), that theorists themselves are people, and that the relationship between theory and practice must take into account the fact that the theorist, the practitioner, and the client are all persons-in-relation. As Hunt and colleagues noted in earlier work (Harvey, Hunt, and Schroder, 1961), behaviors and interactions should be classified by a variety of methods (for example, interviews, observations, and unobtrusive measures). The notion of reciprocal interactions among all three parties must be taken into account and should be used in implementing the theory. As one might anticipate, a consequence of this position is that theories should be revised when inconsistent data are collected in various domains.

Hunt states that proper implementation of a theory must take into account the intentions, knowledge, and competence of the practitioner and the client. It is also important for the theorist to be reflective and responsive to this information. Finally, the theorist must be prepared and willing to apply the theory to him or herself as well as to others. This final suggestion may appear obvious at first glance. Recall, however, what happened to Freud and Jung's relationship when Jung attempted to apply Freud's theory to Freud! (It essentially ended their relationship.)

Tyler (1978, p. 203), in a similar vein, warns us of the dangers of overlooking the issue of individual differences. Studies of differences in creativity, she says, "have made us aware that people do actively deal with possibilities, recognizing, selecting, combining, organizing the voluminous raw material of experience and incorporating the patterns they construct into their own patterns of individuality."

This would appear to be a good point of departure for our discussion of developmental theories of supervision. These theories have been developed by individuals, including ourselves, involved in the practice of clinical supervision. Our ideas concerning the development of counselors and psychotherapists evolved from our experiences as supervisees and supervisors. Our interest in developmental models in general combined with these initial observations to result in our conceptualization of the process in developmental terms. In order to clarify this process, perhaps the impressions of another practitioner/theorist will be helpful.

In discussing the difference between scholars and practitioners, Perry (1977) has described scholars or theorists as being so full of others' ideas that they have no room left for their own. Practitioners, on the other hand, focus so intently on their own ideas that they do not realize that these ideas have already been considered by others. As a practitioner who also theorizes, he suggests that we look at theories as complementary, even if they are logically discrete in their construction. He reasons that no theory is sufficiently robust to encompass all of human behavior, but certain theories may be helpful for given aspects of development. Such a pragmatic view may be at odds with theoretical purists promoting one world view over another, but it fits rather well with positions discussed earlier in this chapter that contend no one model is best or more accurately reflects reality. If the final consideration in evaluating a theory is its utility in various domains, then the pragmatic view has merit.

The purpose of this book is to delineate a model of development that can be used in directing the training of counselors and psychotherapists. The value of this approach, as with any other, lies in how well it serves practitioners and researchers in organizing and integrating knowledge and guiding future research. The model presented in this volume continues the theme of borrowing from existing theories of development to suggest how facilitative change can occur in the training process for counselors and psychotherapists. Concepts are included only when they appear useful in the context of clinical training. Thus, we find ourselves neither completely in the theorist/ researcher nor the practitioner role. Rather, we attempt to reflect the scientist/practitioner model by examining theoretical constructs from a pragmatic perspective. The result, we hope, is a model that will prove useful for both practitioners and researchers in describing, explaining, and predicting changes in trainees over time within the particular domain of clinical supervision.

2

Developmental Models of Clinical Supervision

Supervision of counselors and psychotherapists began with the emergence of psychoanalytic practice between 1925 and 1930 (Leddick and Bernard, 1980). Since that time, a considerable number of approaches to supervision have appeared in the literature. Leddick and Bernard (1980) argue that, even though the literature is extensive, there is no theoretical base for much of the research and writing. They believe that, in lieu of theory, five major orientations—dynamic, facilitative, behavioral, skills training, and blended—have influenced the area. As will be seen, approaches to supervision often mirror approaches used in dealing with clients. A common assumption is that a parallel process exists between counselor-client issues and supervisee-supervisor issues; techniques useful for working with clients are also effective in training practitioners.

In this chapter, we trace important thinking and research in supervision, with a focus on developmental models. These models will be evaluated for strengths and omissions, which will guide the discussion of our own model outlined in the next chapter.

Supervision: History and Context

Ekstein and Wallerstein (1972) described a developmental approach to supervision from a dynamic orientation. They noted three stages in their model that were analogous to a chess match.

14

In the first stage—the opening—the supervisor and trainee engage in initial evaluations of each other's strengths and weaknesses, which lead to attributions of authority and influence. The middle game constitutes a working stage where interpersonal conflicts surface in the form of confrontations, use of defenses (generally on the part of the trainee), and avoidance of issues. During this stage, the supervisor performs the role of counselor and teacher. The final stage—or endgame—marks a shift in supervisor role to less active direction and more silence as the supervisee is encouraged to become more independent.

As we will see, this model differs somewhat from current developmental models of supervision, but it serves to illustrate the historical importance of viewing the process from a structural or stage frame of reference.

With the increasing influence of client-centered therapy during the 1960s and the 1970s, facilitative approaches to supervision emerged. As Leddick and Bernard (1980) note, the early contributions to supervision from this orientation were indirect. Authors most closely aligned with facilitative therapy (Rogers, 1957; Truax and Carkhuff, 1967) suggested that therapist modeling, graded experiences with counseling, and a supportive atmosphere should be the hallmarks of supervision. This was supported by studies that suggested modeling was the most effective form of training (for example, Alssid and Hutchinson, 1977; Gulanick and Schmeck, 1977), that effective supervisors demonstrate empathy, warmth, and genuineness much like effective therapists (Carkhuff and Berenson, 1967; Pierce, Carkhuff, and Berenson, 1967; Pierce and Schauble, 1970), and research suggesting that a focus on personal growth in the trainee was more effective than didactic approaches (Selfridge and others, 1975). Although others noted that the supervision process is actually more independent of the supervisee-client relationship than assumed by this approach (for example, Lambert, 1974), the facilitative orientation prospered and resulted in a more direct application of the approach to supervision. Kagan's (1975) Interpersonal Process Recall Model proposed a structure format designed to allow previously learned counseling skills and information to emerge in the trainee through process recall with the client.

The behavioral orientation also followed a supervision format similar to the focus of therapy. Horan (1972) and Krumboltz (1966) noted that the role of the trainee is to direct clients' behaviors toward specified goals. Leddick and Bernard (1980) note that common practices in supervision within this model centered around training supervisees in specific tasks associated with behavioral therapy (for example, aversive conditioning, counter conditioning, goal setting, systematic desensitization). Thus, learning the procedures one used in behavioral therapy constituted learning the process of supervision. Individuals became proficient by being an apprentice to an experienced therapist, continuing instruction in learning theory, ongoing training in techniques, role-playing, and supervised sessions with clients.

Leddick and Bernard (1980) suggest that the growth in importance of cognitive psychology facilitated collaboration among the dynamic, facilitative, and behavioral orientations, and this resulted in new approaches to supervision. The skills training and blended models emerged as hybrids of these three theoretical perspectives.

The most influential skills training model was proposed by Ivey and others (1968); this model had as its core a communication skills laboratory where trainees would learn specific skills in limited and focused training segments. Hackney and Nye (1973) presented a similar model that focused on "necessary" counseling skills. Modeling of skills and techniques by the supervisor and the teaching of learning theory were the primary mechanisms for both approaches. The skills training model spawned research that both supported and criticized the approach. A number of studies reported that skills training approaches were more effective than a facilitative model of supervision (Cormier, Hackney, and Segrist, 1974; Payne and Gralinski, 1968; Payne, Weiss, and Kapp, 1972; Payne, Winter, and Bell, 1972). Other studies suggested that these learned skills might not transfer well to other counseling situations (Spooner and Stone, 1977) and might decay over time (Mahon and Altmann, 1977; McCarthy, Danish, and D'Augelli, 1977).

Kell and Burrow (1970) proposed a blended model. They

note that this approach incorporated a dynamic theoretical influence, promoted a facilitative style, and used behavioral terminology. In this approach, the supervisor is viewed as a therapist when helping the trainee deal with conflict and anxiety, as a teacher in identifying the sources of these conflicts, and as a consultant for advanced trainees who are able to determine their own goals for learning. This model describes supervisory roles (that is, teacher, therapist, and consultant) that are characteristic of recent developmental models of supervision, which will be reviewed later in this chapter.

Leddick and Bernard (1980) conclude that, while there are a number of consistencies between the models of supervision they reviewed, some issues were neglected by these approaches. An important omission was the process of criticizing or providing feedback to the trainee. Specific issues related to this topic included pairing feedback to the trainee's level of competence and understanding, attending to the trainee's emotional and cognitive needs while timing feedback, and suggesting different methods of conveying feedback based on supervisee characteristics. Other important omissions concerned the need for, or lack of, clarification of the training process for supervisors prior to engaging in supervision and the evaluation of supervisors. To varying degrees, these omissions have been addressed by some of the recent developmental models of supervision.

Recently, models of the supervision process have begun to focus on developmental aspects of the training process. Worthington (1987) has found sixteen models that link counselor development to supervision. He notes that most of the models are remarkably similar, which he attributes to commonalities in supervisor experiences, underlying implicit theories of supervision among supervisors, and reliance upon the same early theoretical writings, particularly those of Fleming (1953) and Hogan (1964). As we will see when we review these current developmental models, some are similar to those described earlier in their basic assumption that the theory one uses for supervision should be the same theory used for counseling and psychotherapy. A similar position has been supported by Goodyear and Bradley (1983) in their analysis of points of convergence and divergence in a selected group of theories of supervision. Thus, similarities between the professional development of the trainee and developmental issues of the client are of interest in these models, suggesting a similar framework for both supervision and therapy. This is most apparent in developmental models coming from a dynamic orientation.

Other writers in the developmental supervision literature, however, describe their models as specific to the supervision process and not merely extensions of counseling theory. For example, Stoltenberg (1981) described his counselor complexity model as appropriate for diverse approaches to counseling and psychotherapy, thus providing a guideline for training that stands independent (within certain limits) from specific counseling theories. Similarly, Loganbill, Hardy, and Delworth (1982) presented their view of supervision as an activity distinct from counseling. As Loganbill and Hardy (1983) have noted, supervision may be sufficiently different from counseling to require a model independent of counseling theory. In addition, they suggest that many professionals describe themselves as using an eclectic approach to counseling and psychotherapy. Thus, an independent model of supervision that is sufficiently robust to encompass diverse counseling theories and techniques is needed.

Developmental Models

We present and evaluate seven developmental models of supervision using a framework suggested by Bartlett (1983) for categorizing supervision models. The selection of models, while somewhat arbitrary, reflects key issues in developmental model building. Some of the models use or imply structural or stage characteristics, while others describe a more continuous and linear growth from simple to complex cognitive structures. The selected models represent both early and recent efforts in developmental supervision. Important criteria for evaluating these models include: purpose, including the theoretical base, goals, and relationship dimension; process, including the format, content, and role expectations; specific characteristics, including treatment modality, setting, and client population; and the criteria and procedure for evaluating the supervisee and supervisor (Bartlett, 1983). As suggested in Chapter One, certain criteria are important in discussing developmental models. The sufficiency of the models in describing behavior changes across time and individuals, explanations of why changes occur in the order described, and attention to mechanisms for encouraging change will be examined. In addition, the relative contributions of maturation versus learning, the presence or absence of critical periods, and the inclusiveness and relevance of the models are discussed.

    None of the models in this section specifically discuss the relative contributions of heredity and environment. Of course, all of the models, to varying degrees, deal with environmental influences, primarily within the supervision setting itself. None, however, suggest that "therapists are born, not made." Instead, most suggest either implicitly or explicitly that both maturation and learning interact to produce effective counselors and therapists. This maturation process, however, appears largely independent of age considerations, which constitutes a major departure from traditional models of development. Perhaps the fact that many trainees are in their mid-twenties or beyond before entering graduate training reduces the importance of age as a measure of development. Nonetheless, age of the trainee is not mentioned by any of these models as a key aspect of development.

    Hogan. One of the seminal works in the developmental supervision literature was written by Hogan (1964). This brief (two-page) outline of a supervision process predated other works suggesting similar processes and formed the foundation for some of the more current models.

    Hogan proposed and outlined a progression through a four-stage model of development for psychotherapists. The first stage is characterized by trainee dependence on the supervisor. He or she is "neurosis bound," insecure, and uninsightful, although highly motivated. Supervision for Level 1 trainees assumes imitation of the supervisor by the trainee, so teaching, interpretation, support, and awareness training are useful supervisory methods. The Level 2 trainee is characterized by a dependency-autonomy conflict regarding the supervision relationship. The trainee, with fluctuating motivation, vacillates between being overconfident and overwhelmed. Supervisory methods, which still consist of support and exemplification, now add ambivalence-clarification. The Level 3 trainee shows increased professional self-confidence, with only conditional dependency on the supervisor. He or she has greater insight and shows more stable motivation. Supervision becomes more collegial, with sharing and exemplification augmented by professional and personal confrontation. By the time the therapist reaches Level 4, he or she is considered a master psychologist characterized by personal autonomy, insightful awareness, personal security, stable motivation, and an awareness of the need to confront his or her own personal and professional problems.

Although Hogan's model describes characteristics of trainees and supervision at each stage, the brief format limits specifics and detail. In addition, a lack of reference to more formal theories of development leaves the reader wondering why the changes should occur in the specified order. Mechanisms for encouraging change in the trainee are also briefly addressed, but only with reference to general categories of techniques. Any notion of critical periods within Hogan's model must be surmised from his description of the developing trainee and tasks at each stage. His picture of development appears to suggest a continuous process of movement from one stage to the next, although no specific timetable for this development is reported.

The purpose of supervision in this model is to foster the growth of the trainee toward more independent functioning based on acquired skills and insight into the client and the trainee's own person. The supervision process itself appears to be intended for individual supervision of trainees with no specific reference to particular treatment approaches or modalities. The roles of the trainee and the supervisor change over time as development occurs. The trainee moves from student to colleague and the supervisor from expert to consultant. Although general criteria for evaluating the supervision process are suggested, no real specifics are provided.

In short, Hogan's model provided the field with a good outline of what developmental supervision should be. The brief presentation, however, left later theorists with considerable gaps to fill, many of which still remain. Hogan failed to make specific reference to existent theories of development that could serve as a conceptual bridge for his work. Consequently, readers are left without guidance when searching for expanded treatments of the process he described. By tying in developmental theories from other domains, researchers and practitioners could translate similar processes into the supervision setting, thus expanding the descriptive and predictive utility of the model and allowing for subsequent validation or revision. The next model we examine attempted to expand Hogan's ideas by integrating processes delineated in a more general developmental theory.

Stoltenberg. The Counselor Complexity Model proposed by Stoltenberg (1981) used as its basis the outline presented by Hogan (1964). To this outline of counselor development, constructs from Hunt's (1971) Conceptual Systems Theory and the earlier work of Harvey, Hunt, and Schroder (1961) were adapted. The stages of counselor development suggested by Hogan were retained, but additional descriptions of optimum supervision environments were introduced. A theoretical basis for proposed trainee changes over time was proposed, and the supervisor's role was tied to the specific developmental needs of the trainee at each stage. The notion of conflict in promoting development was addressed, and the role of the supervisor in encouraging greater autonomy provided the foundation for this model.

Stoltenberg described the development of the trainee through the dependency stage, dependency-autonomy conflict, conditional dependency stage, and finally to the status of master counselor. To the descriptions of supervisee characteristics, Stoltenberg added clarification for supervisory methods, drawing heavily from cognitive developmental theory. Thus, for the dependent Level 1 trainee, the supervisor uses techniques consistent with encouraging autonomy in the trainee while providing sufficient structure to control trainee anxiety. For the dependency-autonomy conflict of Level 2, the supervisor should

provide a highly autonomous environment, imposing less structure on the supervision process. For Level 3—conditional dependence—supervision relies on structure provided by the trainee
rather than by the supervisor. The trainee is largely autonomous
at this point. For the master counselor, supervision becomes
collegial if it is continued at all.

Stoltenberg highlighted Hunt's (1971) and Harvey, Hunt,
and Schroder's (1961) concepts of matching trainee development to particular environments that would provide sufficient
support while encouraging growth toward increased complexity
and greater autonomy. He suggested general supervision techniques for each stage that moved from providing a highly didactic and supportive environment through increasingly greater use
of sharing, confrontation, and mutual exemplification. The end
state, as with Hogan's model, described an independently functioning master counselor who relies on collegial consultation
when necessary.

Within the general guidelines for providing facilitative
supervision environments for trainees at various levels, Stoltenberg translated Hunt's (1971) recommendations for teaching
skills into additional skills necessary for supervisors. Discrimination skills are those necessary for assessing which environments
are most suited to a particular trainee's level of development.
The needs and the strengths of the supervisee must be adequately assessed in order for the supervisor to be able to provide the
optimum environment. In addition, idiosyncratic differences
among trainees must be recognized, with particular attention
paid to the cognitive orientation (conceptual level), motivational orientation regarding preferred type of feedback, particular values of the trainee, and sensory orientations (such as preference for observational learning or Socratic discussions). Finally,
the supervisor must be skilled in creating the various environments required by trainees at different stages of development.
Although a considerable number of guidelines were suggested
by Stoltenberg, specifics regarding various treatment modalities
and the evaluation of supervision were left largely unaddressed.
In addition, adequate training of supervisors remains vague. Still,
the work provided an initial attempt at integrating the develop-

mental process of supervision with theoretical constructs from more formal theories of development. In addition, the work served as a guide for later research on the supervision process.

Littrell, Lee-Borden, and Lorenz. Although similar to the models of Hogan and Stoltenberg, Littrell, Lee-Borden, and Lorenz's (1979) model was based on an integration of four existing models of training for counselors: teaching, counseling/therapeutic, consulting, and self-supervision. All four models were seen as useful for various tasks that trainees must master to become competent professionals. General theories of development were not used to guide the new model. Rather, the four existing models were combined into a sequence that was then described as developmental. The four models of supervision, then, described how supervisors encouraged change in the trainees as the trainees assumed greater responsibility for learning as they progressed through the stages. There are four stages in this model.

Stage 1 consists of establishing a nonjudgmental and supportive supervisory relationship, exploring and setting goals, and developing a learning contract reflecting criteria for competency. These criteria include three critical questions: Where are we going? How do we get there? How will we know when we have arrived? Stage 2 consists of a counseling/therapeutic model focusing on the trainee's thoughts, feelings, and actions in order to overcome a therapeutic block. In addition, specific skills in conceptualization and counseling are taught. Stage 3 is more consultative, where goals are set by the trainee and self-evaluation is encouraged. Finally, in Stage 4 the counselor is self-supervising.

Specific critical periods of development were not fully delineated, but research was suggested to assist in identifying various incidents for specific counseling orientations. However, a continuous model of development was implicit for all approaches.

As with Stoltenberg's model, the Littrell, Lee-Borden, and Lorenz model followed a format consistent with stage theory developmental models, although no formal developmental theory was alluded to in their work. In addition, each stage emphasized procedures used in listening skills training and behavioral approaches. Many of the specifics for particular goals and evaluation processes were omitted. In addition, no reference was made to the notion of various domains in which development may occur. This constitutes a fundamental difference between Littrell, Lee-Borden, and Lorenz's model and the one presented by Stoltenberg. Although little mention of different domains of development appeared in Stoltenberg's original work, his reliance on more formal theories of development implicitly suggested that development will not only occur at different rates for different trainees but will also occur respective to different areas of performance.

As with most of the models we will examine in this section, Littrell, Lee-Borden, and Lorenz's work was limited in addressing a complex process by its brevity. Their work was not clear about the transitions a trainee goes through in the developmental process, and the specific characteristics of trainees delineated for each stage were limited in scope. Individual differences in trainees and the form these differences may take were left largely unaddressed.

Ralph. Another model that appeared at about the same time as the Stoltenberg and the Littrell, Lee-Borden, and Lorenz models was proposed by Ralph (1980). Using interviews with graduate students and supervisors in a clinical psychology program, Ralph identified four stages of development. He described the developmental process as movement from performance in the role of a nondirective expert, to adoption of a patient-centered or content-centered approach, to acceptance of a relationship-centered orientation, to the final stage of therapist-centered therapy. Although the description of the constructs differs from the earlier models we have examined, the process of development presented is quite similar. The trainee's understanding increases in complexity at each level, with the result being an insightful awareness of oneself and one's therapeutic impact on various patients. Although perhaps not intended as a value judgment, Ralph saw a progression of his subjects from a commonsense expert role where they structured the interview and gave advice, to a primarily Rogerian orientation where they learned to use open-ended questions within a non-directive framework. The next conceptual milestone was a change into a dynamic interpersonal focus on the therapeutic relationship, involving both the feelings and reactions of the therapist and the patient, with an eventual end point of a therapist-centered psychodynamic orientation. It is less clear what role the supervisor should play in this process other than, perhaps, one of general support and some reflection or interpretation of blocks.

Although Ralph noted some relationship between his work and more formal theories of development (such as Loevinger, Wessler, and Redmore, 1970; Piaget, 1929; and Harvey, Hunt, and Schroder, 1961), he does not apply constructs from these theories to his own model. The process of evaluating supervision is left unaddressed, and various activities or domains of trainee functioning are not identified. The relevant settings for this model appear to be inpatient and outpatient psychiatric facilities, but specific patient types are not identified.

Yogev. The models presented thus far have attempted to address psychotherapist development from beginning to end. Yogev (1982) presented a three-stage model primarily limited to first-year graduate trainees. Stage 1 is role definition, when the trainee internalizes the therapist role and norms, clarifies expectations from supervision, and deals with the process of evaluation. This takes two to three weeks. Stage 2 focuses on skill acquisition, which is both experiential and didactic and consists primarily of intake training and initial counseling sessions. This takes four to six weeks. Stage 3 consists of solidification and evaluation of practice, where trainees have ongoing clients and present interviews in supervision. This stage includes emotional-experiential, didactic, and skill-practice aspects of supervision.

This eclectic model of supervision focuses on understanding client problems, acquiring necessary skills and techniques, and gaining self-understanding of the trainee's own feelings and behaviors. Although professing, to a degree, a psychodynamic orientation, the model focuses more on delineating a specific program for beginning trainees than it does on describing developmental processes experienced by trainees.

The model lays out a program of training for first-year therapists, breaking down the various stages into periods of weeks and suggesting individual and group supervision guidelines for evaluating progress. The suggestions remain only guidelines, as specifics for evaluating progress are left unclear. Changes in the trainees are presented in a manner that suggests uniform development over a relatively short period of time. Although Yogev notes that the rate of development for later stages will be more idiosyncratic than for earlier stages, she appears to propose that this process should be completed within the first year.

Issues similar to those addressed in previously discussed models—such as dependency, skill acquisition, and resistance—can also be found in Yogev's work. Her goal is independent functioning, although she suggests that this is only initial preparation for later therapist development. Yogev defers to specific orientations and client populations in considering development past the end point of her model. She apparently believes that insufficient commonalities exist among these orientations to allow for consistent stages in subsequent development. Although the discussion of the uses of individual and group supervision is helpful, the model is limited due to its focus on entry-level trainees and provides little direction for conceptualizing later development.

Loganbill, Hardy, and Delworth. The most detailed model we examine in this section was proposed by Loganbill, Hardy, and Delworth (1982). Based on Erikson (1963, 1968), Mahler (1979), and Chickering's (1969) developmental models, Loganbill, Hardy, and Delworth describe the development of trainees over time around specific issues. Three stages—stagnation, confusion, and integration—are sequentially experienced by trainees for each of eight different content issues: competence, emotional awareness, autonomy, theoretical identity, respect for individual differences, purpose and direction, personal motivation, and professional ethics. Among the models we have examined thus far, this work is most explicit in describing different domains of development for psychotherapy trainees. They go on to posit that trainees will recycle through the three stages for these issues in ever deepening levels.

Loganbill, Hardy, and Delworth provide helpful elaboration of various aspects of the supervision process. For example, they enumerate four supervisory functions: monitoring client welfare, enhancing growth within stages, promoting transition from stage to stage, and evaluating the supervisee.

The developmental stage theory they describe relies heavily on accurate assessment. They note that the supervisory context consists of four elements: the supervisor, the supervisee, their relationship, and the environment. Assessment of supervisee variables includes the eight supervisory issues noted earlier plus identification of the developmental stage of the trainee for each of these issues. The first stage, stagnation, consists of naive unawareness in the beginner, or "stuckness" for an experienced counselor. Stage 2, confusion, is characterized by instability, disorganization, conflict, and fluctuations as well as confusion. In addition, the trainee desperately seeks equilibrium while experiencing ambivalence. This unfreezing of attitudes, emotions, and behaviors makes possible movement into Stage 3, or integration. Here a refreezing occurs, indicating a new conceptual understanding, reorganization, flexibility, and security.

Discussion of each of the three stages includes consideration of attitudes toward the world, the self, and the supervisor, in addition to a delineation of the value of each stage for the trainee. Guidelines for qualitatively assessing trainees are provided, as well as suggestions for assessing the supervisory relationship and the environment. An additional strength of the model is the discussion of supervisor variables, which include genuineness, potency, optimism, courage, sense of time as a gift, sense of humor, capacity for intimacy, openness to fantasy and imagery, and capacity for respect and consideration. Also discussed are issues concerning the training of supervisors.

Reference to more formal theories of development allows for clarification of the process of development through the sequential stages proposed in this model. Specific categories of interventions for the supervisory process are presented, and suggestions for their use with trainees at various stages are provided. Specific transition points between stages are noted, and it is suggested that emotional responses are typical between Stages 1 and 2, while the transition between Stages 2 and 3 is more cognitively oriented. The supervisory relationship in this model changes over time as the needs of the trainee and the issues change. The format for supervision appears to be primarily individual or one-to-one. It is implicit that the model is applicable across treatment modalities and client populations.

The monograph format for the presentation of this model allows the authors to address in more detail the evaluation component of supervision. They discuss the value and the problems of evaluating trainees in a threatening environment and the need to address issues openly in order to encourage trust and foster development. The process of assessing stage levels for the trainee based on the predominant issues coming up in supervision provides a guideline for supervisors on implementing the model. In addition, the authors consider the impact of supervisor variables, as well as relationship and environmental variables.

This particular model provides the most detailed consideration of the developmental process for counselors. It may be, however, that it confuses issues with the developmental process. For example, issues of emotional awareness, autonomy, and personal motivation may interact with other domains of practice (such as mastery of different skills, treatment modalities, and client populations) rather than functioning as relatively independent areas of development. In addition, we question whether the recycling concept is necessary. Perhaps what appears as recycling through the same issues is actually more akin to the amoeboid movement of personality development noted by Loevinger (1977) in Chapter One. Also, the apparent recycling may actually be a function of insufficient integration of the developmental tasks for a specific domain with the individual's personal identity.

Blocher. The final model examined in this section was proposed by Blocher (1983). His earlier work in developmental counseling (Blocher, 1966) led naturally to the application of developmental principles to the process of supervision. He notes the purpose of supervision as the acquisition of new and more complex schemas to be used in understanding behavior and interactions. Thus, we again see a proposed movement toward greater complexity and differentiation characteristic of other developmental models. Blocher describes a continuum of development of trainees over time and suggests specific supervisor techniques for encouraging the conceptual development of the trainees. He does not, however, describe discrete stages through which trainees progress. Rather, the developmental process is viewed as a continuous progression from concrete to abstract and complex schemas. The supervisor is urged to use challenge, involvement, structure (a learning contract), feedback and to encourage innovation and integration by the trainee.

The supervision relationship is described as one of mutual trust, respect, and concern for the trainee on both the professional and personal levels, which is consistent with the previous models. Honest feedback is stressed as crucial for conveying trust and respect. In this model, the supervisor assumes the expert role and, apparently, maintains this stance throughout the supervisory relationship. Generally, understanding content, acquiring skills, and achieving personal growth appear to be the desired outcomes of this supervision model. Evaluation is formal, based on collaboratively developed performance standards for the trainee and goal attainment scaling. Various formal developmental theories reflecting a person-environment orientation are referred to. However, little additional clarification of the translation of these theories to supervision is offered.

Upon first reading, the model appears to provide considerable guidance for the supervision process. However, the presentation is so brief and general that little guidance is, indeed, provided. Quantitative differences among trainees are emphasized, and qualitative differences are slighted. Numerous techniques and processes are mentioned, but little integration of these is presented. Blocher's focus on the environmental aspects of supervision, however, is nicely done and provides a framework for additional model building and research.

Summary. The models reviewed in this section are strikingly similar in their treatment of the supervision process using a developmental framework. The various models differ in their inclusiveness, as some detail more adequately changes across time and in individual trainees. Six of the seven models use stages to classify characteristics and processes, but explanations of why these characteristics and processes change in the order suggested by the authors are not adequately detailed. Those models using developmental theories from other areas are more complete in this regard. Virtually all of the models largely describe development as a continuous process that begins with the use of simple or concrete constructs or schemas by the trainee and moves to more complex and abstract conceptualizations applied by autonomous counselors and psychotherapists. The importance of relationship factors for the supervisee and supervisor is implicit in all models, while being explicitly discussed in some. Finally, all of the models suffer from lack of detail and specification of processes, although the Loganbill, Hardy, and Delworth (1982) model is more complete. This brevity of presentation is likely a function of the space limitations imposed by the journals in which the models appeared. The monograph format of the Loganbill, Hardy, and Delworth work allows for greater expansion of ideas.

Empirical Evidence

Although developmental models of supervision are relatively new, evidence is accumulating to suggest the validity of this method of conceptualizing the supervision process. We now briefly review some recent studies that have tested some of the tenets of these models. These studies, as well as others, will be dealt with in more detail in subsequent chapters when specific characteristics of trainees at various levels of development are discussed.

Miars and others (1983) examined the validity of Stoltenberg's (1981) Counselor Complexity Model by asking supervisors to rate perceptions of their own behavior when supervising first, second, and advanced practica students and doctoral interns.

The intent of the study was to see if supervisors perceived any differences in how they conducted supervision with students of various levels of experience. The results indicated significant variations between two levels of trainees—second practicum and advanced practicum. The supervisors noted that they stressed support, teaching, active direction, and close monitoring of trainee clients for less experienced trainees. For more advanced trainees, less direction, structure, teaching, and support were perceived as necessary. Supervisors saw themselves placing more importance upon issues related to the advanced trainee's personal development, dealing with client resistance, and issues of transference and countertransference.

Reising and Daniels (1983) tested constructs from Hogan's (1964) model of supervision by surveying 141 counselors from twenty university counseling centers. They grouped their sample into premasters, masters, advanced masters, and Ph.D. counselors. They noted that trainees in the premasters and masters groups reported being more anxious, more technique-oriented, more dependent on their supervisors, and less ready for confrontation in supervision than the more advanced counselors. The Ph.D. counselors reported being more independent than the advanced masters counselors, who reported being more independent than the less experienced groups.

Hill, Charles, and Reed (1981) conducted the only longitudinal study to date addressing issues relevant to developmental models of supervision. They followed twelve students through their graduate training in counseling psychology, collecting brief counseling work samples at various times and conducting in-depth exit interviews. They reported finding some improvement in skills over time as reflected by use of minimal encouragers and asking fewer questions during sessions. At the exit interviews, the students generally reported having noticed increases in confidence, reduced tendencies for becoming over-invested in their clients, and increased abilities to focus on their clients, as opposed to themselves, over the course of their training. They also noted that they had become more relaxed and spontaneous during counseling sessions and were more able to act naturally with their clients. All of the trainees reported decreased levels of anxiety in dealing with clients as their experience level increased. The trainees' views of their supervisors also changed over time, from seeing them as experts in an evaluation role, to viewing them as consultants, with primary responsibility for clients belonging to the trainees.

Heppner and Roehlke (1984) reported a series of three studies designed to test developmental models of supervision. The combined results of these studies indicated that beginning trainees wanted the supervisor to provide skill training and support more than did more advanced trainees. The focus on skills training that correlated positively with supervision satisfaction varied from level to level, with beginning trainees preferring training in conducting intakes, advanced practicum students desiring skills in alternative conceptualizations of clients, and the interns preferring to focus on personal issues affecting their therapy with clients. The trainees also reported critical incidents in their supervision experiences. For beginning and advanced practicum students, the incidents revolved around issues of support and self-awareness. For interns, the critical incidents were related more to personal issues and their own defensiveness in therapy.

Worthington (1984) conducted a survey of 237 counselors at eleven agencies. He classified his sample into first, second, third, and fourth practicum and predoctoral interns. He found certain factors on his survey instrument that differentiated levels of supervisee experience. Important factors identified were independence with direction, infrequently taught skills, direct monitoring of cases, and establishment of goals. Generally, the trend was to promote increasing independence in trainees as they gained experience in counseling.

Finally, McNeill, Stoltenberg, and Pierce (1985) reported the responses of ninety-one trainees grouped into three levels of experience to an instrument designed to tap differences in supervisees' perceptions of themselves both in supervision and counseling. The results indicated that, as levels of experience increased, trainees tended to report increasing levels of self-awareness and knowledge of counseling skills, and less dependence on the supervisor, with more desire for autonomy in counseling and supervision.

Taken together, these studies provide initial support for a developmental conceptualization of the supervision process. While the evidence is less than conclusive and the studies have methodological drawbacks (such as the general cross-sectional nature of the research), many key constructs of developmental models have received support. For research to advance in this area, the models of psychotherapist development need to be further refined and better articulated. All of the models discussed in this chapter suffer from overly simplified presentations that lack the elegance to describe and predict trainee development in its full complexity. In the next chapter, we begin the process of delineating an integrated model of counselor development that will, we hope, be more robust in its ability to describe and explain changes over time and to promote trainee development.

3

A New,
Integrated Approach
to Supervising Trainees

In Chapters One and Two, we examined basic constructs of developmental theory and models of clinical supervision that explicitly or implicitly utilize these ideas. We now turn to our own reformulated model, the Integrated Developmental Model, or IDM. In proposing this model, we hold ourselves accountable to the criteria proposed by Bartlett (1983) and others for evaluating models of supervision. We will deal with the purpose, process, specific characteristics, and explanations of why changes occur in the order described, with some attention to mechanisms for encouraging change. In later chapters, we discuss evaluation, training, and context in greater depth. Throughout, we offer ideas, data, and examples in support of the relevance and inclusiveness of the model. Conclusive evidence of the latter, however, awaits the judgment of scholars and practitioners in the field.

We adopt the definition of clinical supervision proposed by Loganbill, Hardy, and Delworth (1982, p. 14) as "an intensive, interpersonally focused, one-to-one relationship in which one person is designated to facilitate the development of therapeutic competence in the other person." We also agree with the components of supervisory responsibility for trainee development and evaluation and for client welfare discussed by these authors.

Our model utilizes constructs from developmental theory and from previous developmental models of supervision. We have also incorporated relevant research into the present model. Where research is lacking, theoretical constructs are presented in as much specificity as possible to allow practitioners and researchers to test the validity of such constructs.

The primary basis for the current model is the work of Hogan (1964), Stoltenberg (1981), and Loganbill, Hardy, and Delworth (1982). Empirical studies testing these (and other) models serve as guides for further explication of the model. In addition, recent work in interpersonal influence processes is integrated into the developmental framework in order to suggest mechanisms by which supervisors can influence their supervisees. In line with suggestions by developmental theorists noted earlier in this work, aspects of both the mechanistic and organismic views of development are integrated into the model. Generally speaking, techniques and assumptions consistent with a mechanistic orientation appear within each level of development, while the overall model more closely follows an organismic or growth orientation.

The present model retains the four levels of development suggested by Hogan (1964) and Stoltenberg (1981). However the last level—Level 3 Integrated—is conceptualized as an integrative stage, which results from a natural unfolding from within rather than from structural change per se. The trainee is described as progressing in terms of three basic structures—self- and other-awareness, motivation, and autonomy—in a continuous manner through Levels 1 to 3. This progression is assumed to proceed in a relatively orderly fashion through various domains of functioning relevant to professional activities in counseling and psychotherapy. In each stage, a structural shift occurs across domains. In a spirit similar to the Loganbill, Hardy, and Delworth (1982) model, eight domains are identified as important to professional development. While this list is not comprehensive, it includes activities commonly associated with the training of counselors and psychotherapists. Progress through stages within each domain is assessed by monitoring changes in the three primary structures previously listed. Level 3 Integrated is viewed as integration of domains, which signifies attainment of the fully functioning stage of counselor development.

Overriding Structures	*Specific Domains*
Self- and other-awareness	Intervention skills competence
Motivation	Assessment techniques
Autonomy	Interpersonal assessment
	Client conceptualization
	Individual differences
	Theoretical orientation
	Treatment goals and plans
	Professional ethics

In our model, the levels are conceptualized as a sequence that individuals move through in a fairly systematic fashion. This development is, in Loevinger's (1977) terms, "a bit loose and inconsistent" and follows her concept of amoeboid movement in which an "island" of higher-level functioning expands until the new structure becomes predominant. (See Chapter One for a further discussion of this phenomenon.) Vertical development, or movement ahead to the next level, is explicitly stressed, but the model in practice also attends to issues of horizontal development across domains. While we view the levels as representing irreversible structural change, the model allows for brief regressions when trainees are faced with new or ambiguous tasks. For example, the trainee who has moved to a comfortable autonomy with her or his supervisor may demonstrate a return to dependence briefly when confronted with an unfamiliar client problem. This does not represent recycling through earlier structures per se but is a temporary lapse and movement back toward more familiar territory. It is similar to Piaget's examples of the formal operational adolescent who, under stress, uses the concrete operations of an earlier age. Earlier levels of development do not disappear; they are built upon and left behind but remain available when needed.

Upward movement is seen as occurring as a result of the twin processes of assimilation and accommodation. Utilizing Piaget's constructs (1970), assimilation is the basic process by which we integrate new data into our pre-existing psychic structures. We take information in and make it fit. When this doesn't work, it is necessary to loosen old constructs and build new constructs, or assimilations. This process of modification or transformation is accommodation. Clearly, these two processes work in tandem; both must occur for growth and development. In our model, data that do not fit well in terms of current structures provide the push needed for assimilation and accommodation to occur. The "push and pull" of this process is constant and results in the slow forward movement best described by Loevinger's amoeboid concept.

How, then, do we describe counselors at the three levels of development? Level 1 counselors can be seen as accommodators in relation to their supervisors but as assimilators with their clients. They are characterized by their extreme self-focus and attendant difficulties in hearing their client's view. In Level 2, counselors tend to overaccommodate clients, losing for a time their own ability to assimilate or form their own structures. With the supervisor, trainees may exhibit overly tight assimilations, often evinced as a premature independence in which they focus almost exclusively on their own view. The confusion and struggle of Level 2 may well be viewed as a conflict between overaccommodation and overassimilation. In Level 3, the two processes of accommodation and assimilation begin to work in a more reciprocal fashion, and new data can be accepted and utilized to develop more complex assimilations.

Interactions of Structures and Levels

Our model uses changes in three structures—self- and other-awareness, motivation, and autonomy—to trace the progress of trainees through three different levels. What is the relationship between the levels and the structures?

Self- and Other-Awareness. Level 1 for this structure reflects the trainee's primary focus on him- or herself. This self-focus, which has both a cognitive and affective component and is not particularly insightful, results from apprehension regarding the evaluation by the supervisor and the client. The anxiety common in this stage tends to induce the trainee to focus on his or her own fears and uncertainties, making it difficult to "be with" or understand what the client is experiencing.

One of us recalls working with a beginning trainee who complained that he had difficulty coming up with insightful reflections with his clients. By the time he figured one out, the client would have moved on to other issues. This demonstrates a difficulty for Level 1 therapists. The predominant self-focus, while a necessary phase of development, directly interferes with the trainee's ability to empathize and understand the client.

As Level 1 trainees gain experience, they begin to understand the impact on clients of various techniques. By gaining experience and confidence in rudimentary skills, the trainee experiences less distracting anxiety and begins to understand how techniques or concepts describe and facilitate the therapeutic process in a given domain.

At this point, the trainee (now Level 2) begins to focus more on the emotional and cognitive experiencing of the client. In extreme cases, the trainee may actually lose him- or herself while focusing on the client and become engrossed in the pain, depression, or even elation the client is experiencing. Similarly, by trying to view events from the client's perspective, the trainee may become as confused, optimistic, or pessimistic as the client. As the trainee gains experience, he or she becomes aware of the impact the client has on the counselor, although this information does not fully mitigate the effect.

The Level 3 counselor builds upon the realization of the client's emotional impact on him- or herself and the understanding of how certain behaviors or techniques affect the client. The trainee begins to move back and forth between a focus on his or her own emotional and cognitive responses to the client and an awareness of what the client is experiencing. This ability to move back and forth allows the counselor to integrate information from both perspectives and develop a deeper and more integrated understanding of the concepts relevant to the particular task and situation. It represents the productive use of the dual processes of accommodation and assimilation.

Motivation. The Level 1 trainee generally exhibits a high degree of motivation toward the activities associated with becoming a psychotherapist. This motivation is not based on an in-depth understanding of the role of the counselor or the process of counseling. Rather, it reflects the trainee's intense desire to become a counselor. In most trainees, the desire to help people is present and may interact with the motivation to become whatever model of psychotherapist serves as the ideal for a given individual. The motivation is characterized by a strong desire to learn the "correct" way to counsel and share this new-found knowledge with clients. Often, early success in working with predominantly adequately functioning clients results in a measure of confidence and reinforces the trainee's career selection.

The Level 2 trainee begins to sense that counseling and psychotherapy are, perhaps, not fully powerful or easily learned. Trainees who have developed fundamental relationship skills and have begun the process of developing a more sophisticated understanding of the counseling process are generally assigned clients with more severe pathology than those assigned to beginning therapists. The Level 2 trainee soon finds that he or she may lack sufficient skills and conceptual clarity to work successfully with all clients. In addition, the trainee at this level is usually not protected as much by the supervisor and may be pushed more to come up with his or her own answers to counseling questions. This changing experience tends to result in fluctuating motivation on the part of the trainee. Uncertainty regarding therapy in general and one's own aptitude for the practice can adversely affect motivation to learn and work with diverse clients. At other times, however, success in the process of particularly favorable feedback will bring back the confidence and motivation.

The Level 3 trainee has weathered the Level 2 storm, and motivation is again becoming more consistent. This is a function of learning idiosyncratic strengths and weaknesses, understanding the limitations of counseling and psychotherapy, and integrating a therapeutic style with one's individual identity. This deeper self-knowledge and professional knowledge allows the counselor to acknowledge strengths and limitations in his or her own practice of psychotherapy. Thus, motivation is less likely to be adversely affected when the therapist is confronted with a client with whom successful work is improbable. Referrals can be made without feeling like a failure.

Autonomy. As with anyone entering a new field of practice, the beginning Level 1 counselor is characterized by dependence on authority figures. Knowing little about necessary skills and, perhaps, knowing little about oneself elicit a strong need to be advised by experts. Thus, the Level 1 trainee generally chooses to leave most important decisions up to supervisors or others and will seek advice on numerous issues on a regular basis.

Initial success in counseling activities brings about a stronger desire for some autonomous functioning in Level 2 trainees. This generally results in a dependency-autonomy conflict as the trainee at certain times wants to be treated as an independent therapist, while at other, less confident times he or she wants to be dependent upon the supervisor.

Successful resolution of the previous conflict produces a Level 3 therapist with confidence in his or her ability to function autonomously. When in doubt regarding a particular situation, this person seeks out knowledgeable individuals for consultation without giving up primary responsibility for final decision making. This counselor does not feel he or she is losing face by seeking out advice but will also generally not accept such advice uncritically.

Interactions of Structures and Domains

As we describe trainees at different levels of development in subsequent chapters, we will address in detail how our three structures of interest manifest themselves in the various domains. For the present, however, we focus on some general characteristics of this process and a few specific examples. Our model assumes that trainees may be at different levels in different domains at any given point in time. For example, it is not unusual for a trainee to be at Level 2 in several domains, while clearly being at Level 1 in most. In this section, we limit ourselves to a snapshot of the modal trainee who is operating at one stage for all domains.

The Level 1 Trainee. In all domains, the Level 1 trainee has skills to learn and needs opportunities to practice them. The goal for this trainee is to understand and emulate what occurs when a therapist works with a client. For example, in learning intervention skills a beginning therapist tends to focus on how he or she should perform the skills and when they should be used with clients. The main focus is on the trainee's performance. Such important behaviors as eye contact, posture, and other attending behaviors become an important focus for the trainee. The point is that the trainee is attending predominantly to him- or herself; the trainee's behaviors may lack a definitive tie into the behaviors or needs of the client. Trainees may feel good or bad about their work with a client based on the number of open- and closed-ended questions they ask, with little reference to the effect such questions have on the client.

The motivation of our Level 1 trainee is high across domains. This does not imply, however, a lack of fear or anxiety in these individuals. On the contrary, anxiety plays an important role in stimulating this motivation. The desire of these trainees to become like more experienced therapists provides a strong drive to learn the necessary skills. The theoretical orientation adopted by the beginning trainee often results from emulating a role model. It is interesting to note that often Level 1 trainees have less difficulty providing a one- or two-word description of their therapeutic orientations than do more advanced counselors; this may be a function of selecting a non-ambiguous role model. There is often little question in the minds of beginning trainees as to the sufficiency of a given orientation to work successfully with all clients. The motivation is to learn the approach or the necessary collection of skills, with the understanding that one then will be able to function as a therapist in many different situations. Trainees are eager to learn the "right" way to conceptualize and provide treatment for the client, and they work hard at doing this. Strong motivation is very helpful in fostering the involvement of the trainee necessary for learning relevant skills and interventions.

In any specific domain the Level 1 trainee is characterized by dependence on the supervisor. This is an appropriate response to new situations where one lacks the skills and confidence to perform without careful monitoring. For example, beginning therapists often have difficulty coming up with a comprehensive, or even marginally inclusive, conceptualization or diagnosis of a client. The supervisor is counted on to provide the necessary insights and integration of information for the trainee. When a rather complete conceptualization is provided by the trainee, the supervisor is still depended upon to validate or improve upon the initial effort.

We maintain that these characteristics manifest themselves across the eight domains identified earlier. Specific behaviors, of course, differ since the activities of each domain are somewhat discrete. Nonetheless, the Level 1 trainee is characterized by a predominant self-focus, a strong motivation for learning how to become like other therapists, and a desire to be taught and nurtured by the supervisor.

The Level 2 Trainee. The self-focus of the Level 1 trainee has given way to a focus on the client in trainees at Level 2. A marked increase in the trainee's sensitivity to individual differences is likely to occur at this point. By focusing more on the client, the counselor begins to experience in greater depth the emotional and cognitive states of the client, which broadens the trainee's appreciation for the client's situation. In terms of conceptualizing or diagnosing the client, this trainee, then, knows more about a given client and has a better understanding of the client's idiosyncrasies. This can sometimes prove to be a problem when it comes to classifying the client according to any specific criteria, as the trainee will have worked so hard to take the client's perspective that it may seem too sterile or impersonal to label him or her. As noted earlier, this can also create problems when it comes to understanding how to help a client. The trainee may end up sharing the client's confusion or pessimism and be unable to help the client work through the problems. At times, the Level 2 trainee may not look as advanced in terms of therapy behavior as certain Level 1 trainees. This is not because of developmental regression or incomplete prior learning but reflects uncertainty in response to the greater perceived complexity of the client and his or her life situation.

Given the increased complexity with which the Level 2 trainee is able to approach clients and problem situations, the day-to-day motivation of this individual is likely to vacillate. It is easy to understand how one could lose motivation after a particularly difficult session with a client the trainee does not believe can be helped (at least not by him or her). The trainee may appear unable at times to conceptualize the client or think of appropriate interventions. The domain of individual differences may be the only one that receives consistent and motivated interest from the trainee; there is great motivation to know and understand (accommodate to) the world view of the client.

The dependency-autonomy conflict with the supervisor often is played out in this domain of individual differences. The trainee may become quite resistant to hints that the supervisor understands the client somewhat differently than does the counselor. Resistance is seen across other domains as well. In our experience, it can be especially difficult to work within the domain of professional ethics, where the trainee's overaccommodative stance toward the client can result in poor, if not unethical, judgments and behavior.

The Level 3 Trainee. Vacillations characteristic of the Level 2 trainee begin to subside as he or she enters the third level of development. In terms of self- and other-awareness, this counselor tends to be able to utilize both within the context of counseling. For example, treatment goals and plans reflect the therapist's ability to use a guiding theory or conceptualization of clients and their problems, a deep understanding of how problems are experienced by the client, and sufficient self-knowledge to provide self-assurance that the treatment is likely to be beneficial. In the therapy session, the therapist is aware of his or her reactions to the client and the client's experiencing of emotions and conceptual schemas. The therapist behaves in sessions in a manner congruent with his or her therapeutic orientation, personal style, and goals for the client.

At this stage, the counselor's motivation is more consistent across time. The motivational quality differs, however, from that of our highly motivated beginning counselor in that there is less desire to become like other therapists and a greater need to forge one's own personal identity as a therapist. In terms of intervention skills, the individual is likely to be competent in a number of techniques and general approaches. The issue is which of these are most effective in which situations given the therapist's own personal strengths and limitations.

This movement toward developing an individual therapeutic style is also evident in the therapist's increased autonomy. The therapist does not exhibit the negative independence we usually see in the Level 2 trainee but also does not accept uncritically advice or feedback from others. The Level 3 therapist seeks information and opinions from others when in doubt but evaluates that information in terms of its fit for his or her own orientation, personal style, and impressions of the client. Generally speaking, a lack of defensiveness on the part of the counselor, in addition to an openness to other options, makes this individual an insightful and effective therapist.

The Level 3 Integrated Counselor. The Level 3 Integrated therapist is a fully functioning counselor who has integrated Level 3 skills and knowledge across domains. Thus, this individual functions at a high level in all eight of the specific domains and has the ability to integrate the tasks and products of each domain into his or her therapy practice. This level is not attained by most therapists; persons who do so are often regarded as "master therapists."

This level is also different in that it moves away from the clear linearity of movement in the first three levels and reflects horizontal movement and depth. It represents Piaget's horizontal *décalage,* or unfolding from within, at its best. To a great extent, it represents the ability of a therapist to use all the levels of the past to generate new awareness through dialogue with self and others. Ivey (1986) speaks of the world of "awareness, complexity, and interaction," which well defines for us the world of the Level 3 Integrated therapist. This person is creative, able to learn from self and others, and able to evolve strong and appropriate accommodations and assimilations throughout the life cycle. She or he probably best exemplifies the relational context of supervision of which Gilligan (1982) and others speak.

Additional Considerations

While the levels form the heart of our model and the domains provide an essential context, we believe that attention to additional models and concepts is necessary. Models of interpersonal influence are helpful in approaching the supervisory task, as are concepts relating to gender, ethnicity, and more general cognitive/ego development.

Interpersonal Influence Models. Models of interpersonal influence in supervision have been proposed recently that use the importance and authority of the supervisor in the supervision process. Dixon and Claiborn (1987) and Heppner and Handley (1981) have applied Strong's (1968) interpersonal influence process to the issue of supervision. Briefly stated, these models suggest that perceived expertness of the supervisor and his or her attractiveness and trustworthiness serve as sources of power for the supervisor in producing attitude changes in the supervisee. A related social psychological model of attitude change also provides a framework for examining the function of supervisor credibility. Petty and Cacioppo (1981) have delineated a model of attitude change termed the Elaboration Likelihood Model of persuasion (ELM). This model has been used to expand upon Strong's (1968) interpersonal influence model (see Heesacker, 1986; Stoltenberg, 1986; Stoltenberg and McNeill, 1987).

Applying the ELM to the supervision process gives us some guidelines to follow in encouraging growth in our trainees.

We have already mentioned that motivation is usually quite high in entry-level trainees. In terms of the ELM, this suggests that these individuals will be more likely to engage in what is called central route processing, or the serious evaluation of information provided to them about the process of counseling. Another important determinant of the trainee's likelihood of engaging in this careful cognitive activity is his or her ability to process this information. In terms of the therapy process, limited experience and knowledge regarding counseling and psychotherapy limits the extent to which information provided by the supervisor can be critically evaluated and integrated. Thus, we are likely to find initial acceptance of most of what the supervisor suggests to the trainee, or overaccommodation. This can limit the growth of the trainee if it is allowed to continue for too long a period of time. Thus, it is important that trainees be exposed to numerous orientations and supervisors (if possible) to encourage critical evaluation of information regarding the process of psychotherapy. Although this will induce some confusion, it is necessary to encourage growth and will help the trainee develop the necessary balance between accommodative and assimilative processes.

The opposite end of the continuum of information processing, according to the ELM, is the peripheral route. This approach uses cues from a situation to form an attitude or opinion and decide upon a course of action. Typical cues include the perceived credibility of the source (in this case, the supervisor) and the amount of evidence the source seems to have at his or her disposal (without a critical evaluation of that evidence). Thus, because of the trainee's limited knowledge of the counseling process, he or she becomes vulnerable to peripheral route processing regarding decisions about a client, even though the trainee knows considerably more about the client than does the therapist. The danger here is that the trainee will uncritically accept suggestions and interpretations from the supervisor without adequately attending to the why's and how's of those suggestions. The trainee, in this case, overaccommodates, becoming merely an extension of the supervisor and not an autonomously acting therapist. Little learning can be expected under such situations, and development can be frustrated.

Related Issues. Again, it seems important to remind readers that, while all beginning counselors start at Level 1, the speed of their transitions through levels to some extent depends on the developmental level (that is, cognitive, ego) that they have achieved in their own individual growth. As in any significant new endeavor, the process of learning to be a therapist calls forth a focus on self, an unrealistic high motivation, and dependency, all of which may well have been moved beyond in other areas. For more highly developed trainees, Level 1 should be a very transient experience. Nevertheless, these trainees too must develop in specific domains in order for transitions to new levels to occur. It is our experience that trainees who are more highly developed when they enter a program do indeed move through the levels more quickly; they still, however, experience Levels 1 and 2 before reaching 3.

We also view the levels as being only minimally correlated with age and with experience as a counselor. Many counselors with several years of experience are stuck at Level 1, never having allowed or been exposed to the disequilibrium of new data that do not fit existing cognitive structures. This idea, with some limited empirical evidence, will be discussed more fully in succeeding chapters.

Harvey, Hunt, and Schroder (1961), among others, have issued a caution against equating behaviors with developmental stage. We agree with this, but the assessment problem then becomes even more difficult. For the present, we have outlined a quasi-behavioral assessment approach (see Chapter Seven) as we ponder additional means to investigate the constructs we hypothesize.

Additionally, much developmental literature (see Chapter One) stresses a person-environment focus, with which we concur. The supervisor represents an important environment for the trainee, and this is addressed specifically in succeeding chapters. Ideas about the larger context of supervision are presented in Chapter Eight.

Issues such as gender and ethnicity are important, we believe. Gender, in particular, appears to be salient. As females are generally socialized to be expressive and nurturant, so are males socialized to be instrumental and task-oriented. That such dif-

ferences would not lead to gender-differentiated issues in learning to be a therapist appears implausible, yet little research and
thinking has addressed this issue. Most specifically, we see these
issues arising at Level 2, where females may tend to overidentify
with the client and males may tend to withdraw. We address
this topic in Chapters Five and Ten.

Summary

In this chapter we have proposed a developmental model
of clinical supervision which consists of structural change in
three areas: self- and other-awareness, motivation, and autonomy. We see three levels for each of these structures culminat-
ing in a highly integrated professional level. Development is
basically organismic and linear, with progress occurring in an
uneven, amoeboid fashion. Domains represent eight essential
content areas in which progress occurs. Trainees develop in each
domain using a mechanistic, step-by-step approach, but the integrative point at which "the whole becomes more than the sum
of its parts" is triggered by structural change. The more relational, horizontal, and complex concepts of development come
into play in Level 3 Integrated, which relies not on structural
change but on transformational processes.

The next few chapters look more closely at characteristics of trainees at each stage, with particular attention paid to
the specific domain and the process of supervision. While descriptions of trainees at each level will be used, it is important
for the reader to remember that any given trainee can be at different levels for various domains. We should not make the mistake of assuming that a trainee is at the same level for all domains.

4

Developmental Level One:

The Beginning of the Journey

Level 1 supervisees can perhaps best be viewed as beginners on what their supervisors know will be a long and difficult journey. The trainees are full of trust and hope, and though they know little of what lies ahead, they believe they will eventually become competent—possibly even excellent—counselors.

We can learn much about counselor and psychotherapist development by examining what the trainee looks like coming into training and some of the changes we might expect to witness.

The Entering Student

Students entering training in clinical, counseling, or professional psychology, as well as other mental health professions, are clearly different in personality characteristics and previous experiences. Some students become interested in psychotherapy in undergraduate courses they have taken in psychology or from independent exposure to some of the more prominent practitioners. Given the increased attention of the media to issues of counseling and personality, it is equally likely that a number of entering students first became interested in the profession by reading *Psychology Today* or watching mental health professionals interviewed on television.

Some entering students may have been influenced by successes or failures in advising or supporting others who were experiencing some personal crisis. Finding themselves either effective in helping others, or at a loss as to what to do, can serve as a critical push to enter one of the helping professions.

Still other individuals may have been attracted to the study of professional psychology by their own personal struggles with various problems in living. What better way to learn about oneself than by studying human nature in general? Difficulties with family members or friends who have suffered from emotional problems can serve as an impetus for entering a field of study that offers hope in understanding emotional and behavioral problems.

Needless to say, the motivation for entering a field of study can have important ramifications for later success or failure in the endeavor. Those who want to learn to help others may find themselves initially frustrated by the relative lack of counseling during early points in training and may become disenchanted or bored with the focus on core psychology or experimental design. Both authors can recall a number of incidents when beginning trainees complained to us about the "lack of relevance" of their training and their desire "to help people, not conduct research." By the time our beginning trainees enter the clinic or begin prepracticum training, they are often "champing at the bit" to begin the counseling process.

Motivations for entering the counseling profession aside, criteria for selecting students generally removes some of the sources of variance we might expect among an entering class. For example, the competition for positions in training programs tends to ensure that entering students will largely be a bright and motivated group. Minimally we can expect them to be good students and good test takers. Beyond that, however, programs tend to differ on the relative weight given to prior experiences in selecting students. In very few programs are factors such as maturity or cognitive complexity considered in selecting students. Some programs, in fact, limit their criteria to Graduate Record Exam scores and undergraduate grade point average, with some deference paid to cultural background. Thus, we may know little about a trainee's potential for becoming an effective psychotherapist or an adequate researcher; some of the crucial factors that may affect one's ability to empathize with a client, grasp the complexity of personality and counseling processes, or design and conduct research are unknown.

Can we train anyone with sufficient intelligence to become an effective psychotherapist? Research by Tinsley and Tinsley (1977a, 1977b) suggests that differences may exist in needs, interests, abilities, and personality characteristics between effective and ineffective counselor trainees. Our sense is that many of us who train mental health professionals attempt to guide our students into positions of service delivery, research, or administration based on some criteria for assessing their potential for these activities.

The level of personal development of the individual very likely affects how fast and how far that person will develop as a psychotherapist. In essence, one's personal maturity and cognitive and ego development can be seen as initial limiting factors in his or her early development as a counselor. While certain skills can be taught to most individuals, the effective utilization of these skills and accurate conceptualization of the client and his or her life situation is difficult, at best, for a trainee who lacks sufficient maturity and experience in living. It would, of course, be an error to maintain that one must have experienced a personal crisis similar to those affecting our clients to be able to provide help, or that one must be a "wise old sage" before entering the helping profession to be effective. It intuitively makes sense, however, that past experiences and successful resolution of problems in living can be an aid in understanding and empathizing with a client experiencing a similar difficulty.

Limitations of the cognitive complexity or ego development of a trainee will also affect his or her growth as a therapist. Just as parents cannot expect a five-year-old child to understand the ambiguities of what constitutes right and wrong behavior, a trainee with limited conceptual development will have difficulty grasping the complex interactions of person and environment in the counseling setting. Similarly, a trainee who has not effectively separated from his or her family of origin will have difficulty in helping a client move toward autonomous functioning.

Growth is not a one-way street, however, so we can expect that planned exposure to appropriate learning experiences can help our trainees in their personal development much as it will in their professional growth. Professional development can, and should, encourage personal development. The characteristics that the students bring into the program, however, affect the rate and direction that this growth takes. Adherence to a "supervisee uniformity myth"—comparable to Kiesler's (1966) "client uniformity myth"—serves to deter rather than encourage development. Although our model focuses on common experiences for trainees as they develop, we believe that attention to individual differences remains important.

We now move to a discussion of Level 1.

Level 1 Structures

Stoltenberg (1981, p. 60) describes Level 1 trainees as "dependent on supervisor: imitative, neurosis-bound, lacking self-awareness and other-awareness, categorical thinking with knowledge of theories and skills, but minimal experience." Loganbill, Hardy, and Delworth (1982, p. 17) note that "for the more experienced supervisee, the stage is characterized not so much as naive unawareness, but as 'stuckness' or stagnation."

In terms we have discussed previously, the Level 1 trainee tends to overaccommodate to the supervisor, seeing this person as the all-knowing expert. In contrast, low awareness of others means that many supervisees at this level overassimilate with their clients, that is, they tend to view the client almost exclusively in terms of the supervisee's own previously developed cognitive structures.

Motivation. Level 1 trainees tend to have consistently high motivation, either because they want to do a good job or because they believe they are doing a good job, or both. Anxiety is generally high, but is channeled into hard work, commitment, and enthusiasm for the therapy enterprise. These supervisees are usually consistently attentive and focused on the acquisition of skills. Low motivation is usually characteristic of the more experienced counselor, whose limited self-awareness allows overconfidence, thus resulting in less obvious motivation. Even this trainee, however, perceives him or herself as highly motivated, even when specific motivated behaviors may be absent.

Autonomy. The Level 1 trainee is almost always highly dependent on the supervisor. In the relatively few cases in which this is not true, the experienced counselor who is stagnated will view the supervisor as unnecessary, although still a wise and quasi-omnipotent figure. Level 1 trainees generally want the supervisor to take primary responsibility for the content and direction of supervision. A supportive atmosphere in supervision appears to be highly desired, and trainees prefer positive feedback with minimal direct confrontation.

Self- and Other-Awareness. Awareness of both self and others is highly limited in the typical Level 1 supervisee. This often is a result of a rather low self-concept, in which the student views learning as coming from an outside source. The lack of awareness may also be seen in supervisees who think they are functioning in a competent manner but who are unable to specify their strengths and weaknesses as a counselor/therapist. These students may have a vague sense of working (in a mechanical way) with clients but are not able to understand or specify this sense. Most Level 1 trainees go through a period of intense focus on self. This focus results from anxiety and will not in itself lead to productive self-awareness.

Interaction of Structures and Domains

What, then should we expect of this highly motivated, dependent, and professionally naive trainee? For most trainees, basic Level 1 descriptions are valid. As time passes, trainees begin to function at Level 2 in one or more domains. As the number of domains in which the trainee functions at Level 2 increases, structural changes occur that propel him or her into the general state of ambivalence and confusion characteristic of Level 2.

Intervention Skills Competence. Although this is categorized as a specific domain, it remains in some sense an overarching category. All sorts of skills are necessary for counseling and psychotherapy, as well as for related activities such as consultation and programming. Additional skills are necessary for certain types of clients, as well as for various forms of counseling (for example, marital and family, and group counseling). The specific counseling activity, then, must be considered when assessing skills competence. It would be unfortunate to assume that someone exceptional in individual supportive counseling is also skilled in behavioral marital therapy.

In general, however, the beginning trainee (or the practicing professional with little or no experience in a particular counseling approach) tends to want training in circumscribed skills and looks for a structured format to follow in implementing those skills. This early desire for structure reflects the cognitive self-focus of the trainee. The beginning counselor primarily attends to the "right" way to do things by focusing on her or his mental outline of the intervention strategy. The trainee is so focused on remembering how to utilize an intervention that little attention is left for understanding the client's perspective.

This self-focus also has affective components, as the trainee may often feel anxious or apprehensive. The trainee may lack confidence in his or her ability to perform the intervention or to help the client. This anxiety will be intensified if ambiguity is introduced by the supervisor at this time.

Trainees who have been exposed primarily to one particular school of thought regarding therapy may identify so heavily with that orientation that others are excluded. This is not entirely bad, as it tends to limit the confusion that can attend integrating more than one theoretical approach with specific intervention techniques. If left to her or his own discretion, the trainee often attempts to use the adopted orientation with most clients and, perhaps, in other formats (for example, marital or group counseling) until it is no longer effective. The beginning trainee is likely to feel some early sense of power from mastery of certain counseling skills. Thus, the trainee's motivation to learn more about the counseling process is increased, and usually there will be a strong desire to see clients and practice these skills.

During this early phase, the trainee is highly dependent

on the supervisor for knowledge about techniques and when they should be applied. There is a strong need for positive feedback and a concomitant desire to learn within a supportive environment. For example, one intervention skill that Level 1 trainees often have difficulty learning is that of confrontation; they tend to see their clients as fragile and vulnerable. Supervisors have to be creative in working with the trainee's anxiety both to do well and to care for the client. A highly conscientious Level 1 trainee responded well when the issue was framed in terms of fostering client welfare and discouraging maladaptive behavior.

Assessment Techniques. Work in this area usually begins with course work in assessment instruments or training in intake procedures. Particularly with objectively scored instruments, early trainees are likely to forget that test results indicate the likelihood of certain personality characteristics, cognitive styles, vocational interests, and so on, and not the certainty of these attributes. Heavy reliance on statistical probability in the absence of interview data or, conversely, sole reliance on interview impressions without additional validation from testing may exist. This highlights the cognitive self-focus of the trainee. The theoretical constructs of assessment assume primacy as the trainee tries to fit the client into neatly defined categories. Skills in administering tests, particularly those requiring following up on responses (for example, projective tests), develop slowly as the trainee moves from a rigid performance to a more relaxed approach (while maintaining standardization of procedures). As with intervention skills, in the beginning the trainee is likely to focus more on his or her own anxiety concerning the assessment situation than the client's emotional reactions. Selection of tests and integration of results will mostly be "cookbook" at this stage, with a focus on consistency among results and a tendency to ignore discrepancies. The trainee relies heavily on the supervisor in selecting assessment approaches and interpreting the results.

Interpersonal Assessment. Although this easily could be included under the domain of assessment techniques, it often involves quite a separate process. It is often more akin to counseling skills development, where an individual learns to use him- or herself in the session to elicit responses from the client useful in assessing social skills and personality characteristics. At the beginning of work on this domain, a trainee often either ignores the process or attributes too much pathology to normal responses in anxiety-producing situations. This is a function of the trainee's self-focus and reflects his or her inability to take the perspective of the client. This inability makes it difficult for the Level 1 trainee to respond to unexpected statements and actions of the client. If it becomes difficult to categorize the client, anxiety and uncertainty are likely to ensue. The trainee will then rely heavily on the supervisor to validate the trainee's perceptions or to provide alternative conceptualizations of the process.

Client Conceptualization. Many approaches to *formal conceptualizations of clients* are possible. One we have found useful was proposed by Loganbill and Stoltenberg (1983). We believe that this approach encourages a more complex understanding of client dynamics, as well as integration of relevant data. Beginning counselors often focus on specific aspects of the client's history, current situation, or personality assessment data to the exclusion of other relevant information. Grand conclusions may be based on rather discrete pieces of information, selected for their consistency with a particular theoretical orientation rather than for their salience to the client's presenting problem. This search for consistency reflects the trainee's desire for a simple conceptualization of the client. As noted in the previous section, there often exists a tendency to either "psychopathologize" or "normalize" client conceptualizations. In the beginning, the trainee lacks confidence in his or her ability to accurately conceptualize the client and prefers such diagnostics to be provided by the supervisor. A helpful function of the Loganbill and Stoltenberg (1983) case conceptualization format is that the trainee is directed to collect relevant information across a broad spectrum of the client's experience. The trainee is then required to integrate this information into a conceptualization of the case and the subsequent treatment plan.

Individual Differences. This domain includes both an awareness of sexual, racial, and cultural differences among clients and diagnostic classifications of client disorders. Early trainees often rely too heavily on their own idiosyncratic experiences and perceptions of the world. This can have two different results. Trainees may assume that they share a common phenomenal field with most clients, therefore downplaying the importance of differences in background, culture, and gender. Or trainees may believe that little or nothing is shared with clients of different races, gender, and so on. This second tendency can present a seemingly overwhelming task for the trainee in her or his attempts to empathize with the client. Similar issues can arise with regard to approaches to treating various disorders. One perspective is that one approach fits all diagnoses of client disorder. On the other hand, the trainee may be so overwhelmed by discovery of a "serious pathology" that acquired counseling skills are not used and the trainee becomes immobilized. If the trainee relies primarily on idiosyncratic experiences or on recently learned formal theories, the client is not seen as an important source of information. Empathy is difficult when one focuses primarily on oneself.

Theoretical Orientation. As noted earlier, it is not uncommon for beginning trainees to grab on to a particular approach to therapy with disciple-like fervor. Proficiency with a particular orientation is a laudatory goal; eclecticism, while the norm, is not necessarily to be desired. However, in an attempt to become an expert quickly, the neophyte trainee may rule out a number of counseling techniques or theories in favor of one more easily understood or commonly accepted. This, of course, limits flexibility in responding to clients with various presenting problems, as well as encouraging an early tunnel vision that may limit the trainee's development. For the trainee, however, this early adherence limits confusion and reduces the anxiety that can accompany uncertainty. By taking advantage of the trainee's high level of motivation, the supervisor can promote a good foundation in listening skills and behavioral interventions, which can provide a firm base from which a trainee can branch out. As a matter of convenience, the trainee is in-

clined to learn the supervisor's orientation, as he or she is dependent in the beginning on the supervisor for advice and direction.

   Treatment Goals and Plans. Those who have supervised
beginning therapists (as well as many advanced trainees) have
probably experienced asking the supervisee after four or five
sessions with a client to describe the treatment plan and finding
that none exists. It is difficult for beginning trainees to visual-
ize the process of therapy from intake to termination. Often
beginning trainees are satisfied if they can get their clients to
talk for most of a session and seem unable to devise a plan for
dealing with the client's concerns. How to get from here to
there presents a difficult problem in conceptualizing the counseling process for a specific client. When a trainee writes up a
treatment plan, one may find that the objectives and long-term
goals do not translate well into specific interventions across
time. In other words, the trainee may have certain techniques in
mind but may have neglected to attend to long-term goals or
short-term objectives. On the other hand, the trainee may have
an idea where the client should be at the end of treatment but
have little idea how the client will get there.

   Tying counselor behaviors from particular sessions into
the overall treatment plan can also be an interesting experience.
Quite often the trainee takes therapy one step at a time and
does not consider which particular objectives to pursue during
a given session. Experienced therapists may take the same approach but experience different results. The difference is due to
the fact that the experienced therapist draws on a wealth of information during a session and is likely working from some
type of plan (even if not very well-defined). The beginning
trainee is more likely to be "shooting from the hip" rather than
following a logical course of therapy.

   An exception to the above process, though, may occur
when a trainee is implementing a rather structured treatment
program (for example, systematic desensitization). In this case
the trainee may follow the format in a concise, stepwise fashion
but have difficulty assessing the appropriateness of the approach

over time. The trainee may not pick up information from the client during therapy that could suggest a change of treatment plan.

Professional Ethics. Early training concerning profession-al guidelines for ethical behavior and state laws concerning the practice of counseling and psychotherapy is very important. Rote memorization of these guidelines can occur rather quickly. Integrating ethics with personal and professional values and identity comes more slowly during later stages of development. General ethical guidelines can be adhered to rather easily. Prob-lems occur, however, when details of a specific case or situation give rise to an ethical dilemma. At such times, the supervisor is expected to take charge and decide what should be done. For example, one trainee we worked with was manipulated into meeting with the friend of a client. The trainee, who was un-comfortable in the situation, did not divulge any information but also did not question the meeting until her supervisor asked why she felt she had to see the friend. At that point, the trainee began to explore ethics and professionalism in a broader way.

Empirical Evidence

The beginning counseling and psychotherapy trainee is the focus of most of the empirical literature dealing with the supervision process. This is probably due to the ease with which this population can be studied. Often, more trainees at this level are available than trainees with greater experience. Also, the training processes examined by these studies tend to be the more simple and easily measured ones. Acquisition of initial counseling skills lends itself more readily to analysis than do complex interactions with pathological clients.

Empirical investigations provide some support for our de-scription of beginning counselors. Worthington and Roehlke (1979) found that entry trainees prefer modeling, sharing coun-seling experiences, receiving positive feedback, the existence of structure, and suggestions of literature on counseling effective-ness. Relationship dimensions are also stressed by the trainees.

Similarly, Reising and Daniels (1983) examined 141 practicum students, interns, and professional staff from twenty university counseling centers. They report that trainees with relatively little experience in counseling described themselves as more anxious, dependent, and technique-oriented than more experienced trainees. In addition, they appeared less ready for confrontation. Because both of these studies relied on factor analytic techniques to derive important dimensions of counselor development, differences among groups of trainees at different levels of experience must be viewed with caution. Neither study had a particularly large number of subjects given the high number of items analyzed, which reduces the confidence with which one can generalize from factor analytic studies. Nevertheless, both studies indicate that beginning trainees are very different from more experienced counselors.

A recent study by McNeill, Stoltenberg, and Pierce (1985) investigated some of the differences expected between trainees with different levels of experience using a composite measure of educational, counseling, and supervision experience. Using an instrument designed to measure aspects of Stoltenberg's (1981) model of counselor development, they report differences between three levels of trainees in the degree of reported self-awareness, dependency-autonomy, and knowledge of theory and skills. As expected, less experienced trainees reported less self-awareness, more dependency on the supervisor, and less knowledge of theory and breadth of skills. Another investigation by Stoltenberg, Pierce, and McNeill (1987) looked at the needs identified by trainees at different levels of the same composite measure of experience. The results indicate that beginning trainees believe they have a greater need for supervisor-provided structure and positive feedback than do the more advanced trainees. Based on a composite score of a number of supervisee needs (for example, for structure, instruction, positive feedback, support from the supervisor, and desire for autonomy), beginning supervisees report greater need than do the more experienced trainees (with reverse scoring for autonomy). Similar results for trainee characteristics and needs have been reported in studies looking solely at supervisors' perceptions of their supervisees (for example, Miars and others, 1983; Raphael, 1982; Wiley, 1982).

A recent study by Stoltenberg, Solomon, and Ogden (1986) presented four descriptions of trainees and four descriptions of supervision environments derived from Stoltenberg's (1981) model. The Level 1 trainee description was presented earlier in this chapter. The supervision environment was taken directly from Stoltenberg (1981, p. 60): "Encourage autonomy within normative structure. Supervisor uses instruction, interpretation, support, awareness training, and exemplification; structure is needed." Thirty supervisees and their supervisors were asked to independently choose the trainee description that most accurately described the supervisee and the supervision environment most appropriate for that trainee. The descriptions were not identified as to which were more advanced or reflected higher levels of development. Positive correlations emerged on both dimensions between the supervisees and their supervisors. These ratings also correlated positively with the level of counseling experience reported by the supervisees, indicating that differences in development (as a function of experience) were noted by both trainees and their supervisors.

Perhaps a better description of entry-level trainees than "neurosis-bound" (used by Hogan (1964) and Stoltenberg (1981)) is anxious. A study by Hale and Stoltenberg (forthcoming) investigated reasons why beginning trainees tend to exhibit more anxiety than more experienced trainees. They hypothesized that two factors account for much of the anxiety experienced by novice trainees. One factor is evaluation apprehension. In this case, the fear is of evaluation by the supervisor. The second factor, borrowed from social psychology, is objective self-awareness (Duval and Wicklund, 1972). This factor suggests that the process of being videotaped, audiotaped, or otherwise made to focus on oneself in counseling can elicit negative evaluations of one's performance and concomitant feelings of anxiety. By manipulating whether beginning counselors believed their counseling would be videotaped only, videotaped with critical review by a supervisor, or not videotaped or reviewed, the researchers were able to influence the amount of anxiety reported by the trainees. Those under the videotaped and reviewed conditions reported more self-awareness and evaluation apprehension during the session than those in the videotaped only condition. In addition, the videotaped and reviewed condition elicited the most anxiety of any of the three conditions. Thus, the process of being videotaped and evaluated produced considerable anxiety in these young counselor trainees. No such differences were reported in a similar study by Bowman and Roberts (1979) of more experienced trainees.

The Supervisory Environment

The most important principle in supervising Level 1 trainees is to provide structure to keep the normal anxiety of the trainee at manageable levels. To the beginning therapist, the supervisor is generally an expert in the process of counseling and therapy. He or she is looked to for relevant information about counseling techniques, orientations, client characteristics, and all of the other aspects of the training process. Of course, supervision does not occur in a vacuum. The trainee is exposed to other sources of information in course work, discourse with peers, and so on. The supervisor of beginning therapists should expect to have her or his credibility occasionally challenged as the trainees attempt to integrate different bits of information into a model of the "right" way to do therapy. Generally speaking, though, the trainee views the supervisor as a role model and resident expert.

Changes occur as the Level 1 counselor develops. We noted earlier that this individual at first predominantly attends to his or her own cognitions and affect. Early confusion regarding various constructs relevant to therapy generally evolves into a degree of conceptual clarity for the Level 1 trainee. The early anxiety regarding counseling and supervision also dissipates somewhat as the trainee receives positive feedback from the supervisor and his or her clients. Although the trainee remains largely dependent on the supervisor, this dependency subsides as the level of confidence increases. An intense self-focus, however, limits how well the trainee can judge her or his effectiveness with the client. Thus, the perceptions of the supervisor remain important. The supervisor needs to be sensitive to the growth of the trainee's confidence so that the amount of direction and structure provided by the supervisor can be reduced accordingly. In addition, less reliance on the supervisor by the trainee and increasing skills levels indicate that the trainee is ready for more difficult clients and more complex treatments of the therapy process.

Interpersonal Influence Models. We introduced these models in Chapter Three, with emphasis on the Elaboration Likelihood Model (ELM). This model promotes what it calls central route processing, or the effortful evaluation of information. The beginning counselor is seen as vulnerable to peripheral route processing, that is, use of cues such as perceived credibility of the source (for example, the supervisor). The danger is that the trainee will uncritically accept suggestions and interpretations from the supervisor.

It is, of course, a responsibility of the supervisor to protect the client and monitor the treatment so that progress without undue risk can be expected. This should not, however, translate into taking over the trainee's cases and constantly directing the therapy. To promote growth, autonomy in the beginning trainee must be encouraged. In our own experience as supervisors, we admit that it is often easier to instruct a trainee on what to do than it is to problem-solve with that trainee and assist her or him in deriving a conceptualization or an intervention. Still, if we wish our trainees to function independently at some future time, we must encourage risk taking and central route processing on their part, even though they may resist this push towards autonomy and responsibility. We must provide plenty of opportunities for trainees to observe supervisors and other role models conduct therapy, role-play, and interpret client (as well as supervisee) dynamics.

It is critical that a degree of ambiguity or conflict be introduced in order to create a sufficient (but not disabling) amount of disequilibria in the trainees. Growth is not encouraged if supervision or the experience of counseling becomes too comfortable. Assuming too much responsibility for the trainees' cases can limit their growth by removing too much of the uncertainty or conflict necessary for them to move to higher levels. Balancing support and uncertainty is the major challenge facing supervisors of beginning therapists.

Techniques. Specific techniques useful for beginning trainees are those that provide them with significant information about the progress of psychotherapy. An example of this (as mentioned above) is allowing the trainee to observe the supervisor and other practitioners working with clients. Early attempts at counseling by the trainee often take the shape of imitation. At this stage, that is acceptable and can even be encouraged. Through imitating others, the trainee acquires a number of skills and techniques that can be creatively used in the future. Observing peers conducting therapy can also be helpful. Most trainees have comparable levels of expertise, and it can be instructive to watch someone at a similar level work.

Role playing can also be invaluable in helping the trainee learn and apply new skills in counseling. In group supervision formats, having trainees role-play among themselves can provide a useful adjunct to individual supervision. Case presentations by supervisees in a group supervision setting (particularly if such presentations include videotapes of counseling sessions) can aid in the learning process; considerable vicarious learning can occur through helping classmates conceptualize clients and select interventions.

Interpersonal Process Recall (IPR) (Kagan, 1975) and microcounseling (Ivey, 1971) are structured or programmed approaches to supervision that work well with beginning trainees. In IPR, the trainee goes over the videotape of a session in the presence of the supervisor and the client. Care, of course, should be taken to make this a constructive experience and one not overly anxiety-provoking. Similarly, microcounseling allows for the learning of specific counseling skills in short role-playing segments. This can help the trainee acquire a number of important skills.

Care should be taken in using these or any other approaches to avoid a totally technical orientation to therapy. If flexibility is not introduced into the process, creative application of what is learned is not encouraged.

These approaches can be quite effective for beginning counselors because they do provide structure for the learning process, which tends to reduce anxiety and simplify learning. These approaches may seem stifling to more advanced trainees, and supervisors may encounter resistance.

Structured or programmed approaches to training and supervision are not required; careful attention to the development of the trainee and his or her performance in counseling situations are sufficient guides for deciding upon the format and content of supervision. With help, the trainee can become aware of his or her areas of weakness and strength in counseling. It is usually more productive to first address the strengths and provide positive feedback to the trainee and then go on to the areas where improvement is needed. The uncertainty and anxiety of the beginning trainee can easily turn into defensiveness if the supervisor is considered too critical. Supervisors must not ignore weaknesses or mistakes in therapy because of concern that the trainee is too vulnerable to accept negative feedback. If this becomes an issue, consideration should be given to interrupting the practicum experience for the trainee while counseling for this problem is undertaken. Needless to say, such counseling should be provided by professionals outside of the training program.

A case conceptualization format (such as the one proposed by Loganbill and Stoltenberg (1983)) can be useful in both individual and group supervision. Any tool that helps the trainee attend to diverse sources of information about the client and encourages use of that information in the treatment plan elicits learning and growth. It also serves as a shorthand mechanism for conveying information about clients in case conferences, thus leaving more time for problem solving. Such a format is also helpful in monitoring the case load of trainees. It is the responsibility of the supervisor to monitor treatment and the progress of the trainee's clients. All too often, time in supervision sessions is spent on updates of clients, with little or no learning occurring. This time is too valuable to be used in this way; it should be spent exploring issues in ways that promote the trainee's professional growth.

We recommend using videotaped or live observations of the trainee's counseling sessions rather than relying on verbal accounts or audiotapes. Much information is lost with audiotapes, and (regardless of the trustworthiness of the trainee) verbal accounts of therapy often are not accurate. In marriage and family therapy, live observation of trainees is becoming increasingly popular. Also common are telephone conferences between the trainee and the supervisor during the therapy session in order to provide immediate feedback and guidance to the trainee. A similar approach is the "bug-in-the-ear" technique, where a small receiver is placed in the trainee's ear through which he or she can receive suggestions from the supervisor while working with the client. All of these techniques can be helpful in teaching the process of therapy. Care must be taken, however, to avoid the pitfalls mentioned above concerning the supervisor taking too much control over the therapy session. Hearing the supervisor talking through an earphone or receiving a phone call in the middle of a session can be very disruptive for the trainee. Often, the supervisor may be unaware of the direction the trainee wishes to go with the client and may prematurely push the trainee to go a different route. If such intrusive forms of supervision are used, care must be taken to encourage growth and risk taking in the trainee and to avoid turning the therapist into a mere extension of the supervisor.

Learning Styles. A final issue we want to discuss concerns different learning styles among trainees. Stoltenberg (1981) applied Hunt's (1971) matching model of conceptual complexity to the supervision process. Hunt suggested that the conceptual level of the trainee must be taken into account when creating the appropriate supervision environment. Evidence from the supervision literature supporting this contention has been reported by Berg and Stone (1980). For trainees of relatively lower conceptual levels, more structure is needed to encourage learning of skills and techniques. Even for trainees of relatively high conceptual levels, however, early structure is likely to be helpful in clarifying the counseling and supervision process. Conceptual level is an indication of general cognitive development but may be an inaccurate measure of development within the domain of counseling and psychotherapy (or other related activities). Higher initial conceptual level should, however, increase the rapidity with which a trainee learns and integrates new material. The process of horizontal *décalage* referred to in Chapter Three of this volume suggests this augmented speed of development.

Hunt (1971) also suggested that whether an individual is inner- or other-directed may have important consequences for learning and feedback. Inner-directed trainees may prefer self-defined feedback, while other-directed types may prefer supervisor-defined feedback. Similarly, Bernstein and Lecomte (1979) reported that field-independent counselor trainees were more open to feedback and evaluated it more positively than field-dependent trainees, particularly when the feedback was positive and congruent with their own perceptions. Another study (Handley, 1982) suggested that similarity of cognitive style between the trainee and the supervisor, as measured by the Myers-Briggs Type Indicator, may result in an enhanced perception of the trainee's performance. It is also likely that this will affect how information is presented to and received by the trainee.

Finally, some trainees learn better vicariously, while others seem to need to learn by doing. Providing certain trainees with a reading list of important theories of psychotherapy may be helpful in teaching them to apply different models and techniques, while it may leave others wondering about the relevance of it all. Some trainees learn more easily from verbal explanations than from written ones. Listening to the trainee and monitoring how information is best incorporated provide guidelines for selecting mechanisms for communicating about counseling and psychotherapy. It is important for developmental models of supervision to consider differences in learning styles among trainees (Stoltenberg, 1981). As we have noted above, these characteristics can affect the manner in which supervisors convey feedback and make recommendations to trainees. We should not overlook idiosyncratic differences in learning styles as we guide trainees in their development.

The Next Step

In this chapter we presented descriptions of trainees during their early phase of training that we believe are helpful in supervising such trainees. We tried to strike a balance between presenting useful generalizations and providing sufficient qualifiers to those generalizations to allow for flexible supervision. Not all trainees are alike, and it is an error to treat them all the same. It is, however, an equally grievous mistake to assume that no similarities exist among trainees at any given level of development. It is recognition of both the similarities and the idiosyncrasies that underlies our framework for supervising trainees. By balancing between what we expect to occur and the individuality of our trainees, we can best provide a constructive growth experience for them.

When our trainee has evolved a fairly clear conceptualization of counseling techniques and theory—with a concomitant decline in initial anxiety and increase in confidence—more of a sense of autonomy is evident. In essence, the trainee has consolidated gains and equilibrated at the first level of development. For some trainees, this occurs when they are still beginners in terms of experience. For others, it comes only after several semesters of practicum. For a few, it seems not to occur at all.

At this point, it is essential to facilitate the trainees' transition to Level 2. As we will see in the next chapter, one way to begin is the assignment of more difficult clients. Deeper understandings fostered by the professional training program also contribute. But this process must usually be aided by the supervisor, who provides a more questioning environment for the supervisee. In this transition, the supervisor, while still highly supportive, presents additional confrontations. Our experience suggests that the most effective techniques at this point are affective confrontations focusing on the trainee's awareness of self and client. These interventions may take the form of process comments by the supervisor, highlighting important aspects of the interaction between the trainee and the client or between the trainee and the supervisor. Affective interventions seem to have the most potential for pulling supervisees, albeit unwillingly, toward the necessary ambivalence and confusion of Level 2, which in turn promotes development.

It is our experience that the minority of Level 1 counselors who are "stuck" rather than "naive" require this transition work early in the supervision period. In essence, they have been at Level 1 for some period of time prior to our work with them, and it is time to move on!

It is difficult for many supervisors to stir things up once their students seem less anxious in the counseling situation. Yet the "end of Level 1" trainee is still too unaware, too rigid, and too dependent to be an effective therapist. The unsettling and confusing affect that characterizes Level 2 serves to unfreeze cognition and structures in a manner that allows further development. Some number of practitioners never reach this point. They remain at a level where they use techniques in a mechanical way, never grasp the real essence of the client, and are unaware of their own complex reactions in the counseling interview. Perpetual Level 1 counselors do little good, may do harm, and clearly miss the true joy of doing excellent therapeutic work. Supervisors, therefore, are advised to summon the courage and integrity to begin the challenge that opens the door to Level 2.

5

Developmental Level Two:

Trial and Tribulation

Our entry-level trainee has changed somewhat from the individual we encountered during initial clinical training. The largely dependent, imitative, and unaware trainee who required considerable structure, support, and instruction when first beginning counseling has developed into our Level 2 trainee. Stoltenberg (1981, p. 60) described this counselor as showing "fluctuating motivation, striving for independence, becoming more self-assertive and less imitative." The dependency on the supervisor has given way to a dependency-autonomy conflict. Loganbill, Hardy, and Delworth (1982, p. 18) have called this the "confusion" stage and stress the " 'unfreezing' of supervisee attitudes, emotions or behaviors." Key characteristics of the stage are disruption, ambivalence, and instability. Simply put, this stage can be a trying one for supervisor and supervisee alike!

What has produced this change in the trainee? By the time the counselor reaches Level 2 (for many trainees, this roughly coincides with advanced practicum status), he or she has gained some experience with the process of psychotherapy and has worked successfully with some clients. If the trainee was handled effectively during the first stage of development, most of the clients with whom he or she worked were probably normally functioning individuals suffering from some situational difficulty. Good listening skills and attending behavior accompanied by some rudimentary intervention strategies were likely to be sufficient in dealing with this population. Thus, the trainee will have experienced some successes in the counseling process, and many of the basic counseling skills have been learned.

By now the supervision process has yielded some of the trainee's strengths and weaknesses. Careful attention to recordings of counseling sessions or live observations of the trainee has helped the supervisee to become more aware of her or his own reactions to various clients. In addition, the trainee's impact on clients becomes more apparent, as different interventions and styles of interacting have been attempted and their effects noted. The supervisor has taught various skills, supported the trainee through the trying process of becoming acclimatized to the counseling situation, and helped the trainee become more aware of the interactional nature of counseling.

At this point the trainee begins to realize, on an emotional level, that becoming a psychotherapist is a long and arduous process. The trainee discovers that skills and interventions effective in some situations are less than effective at other times. The student struggles to understand why he or she is successful with certain clients, while at other times little or no progress is forthcoming. This struggle to understand can have negative effects on motivation. During this stage, the trainee may begin to question the effectiveness of counseling in general and the suitability of this career option for him or her in particular.

As the trainee gains more experience with counseling and with the supervision process, idiosyncratic strengths and limitations become more apparent. Of course, increased practice and experience overcome some of the acknowledged weaknesses but others surface as relatively stable attributes of the person. Differentiation of which attributes are skills or conceptual deficiencies and which are stable person variables becomes a major task of supervision. In addition, the trainee begins to understand the limitations of "talking therapy" as a mechanism for dealing with client pathology. What was once clear (or at least unknown) to the trainee now becomes complicated and murky.

An appreciation for the complexity of the counseling process is emerging. The trainee is entering Level 2.

Level 2 Structures

Autonomy. Trainees are more self-assertive. They begin to move away from imitating the supervisor and toward developing their own ideas regarding effective interventions. At such times, the trainee is less inclined to ask for recommendations concerning a particular client and may even resist discussing the progress of therapy if he or she suspects that the supervisor will disagree or suggest alternative approaches. The trainee vacillates between dependency and autonomy. Indeed, reactance or counterdependence may accurately describe the trainee's behavior at some points during this stage. At the risk of oversimplification, one recognizes similarities between counselor development during this stage and child development at around the age of two or three years. The issues, of course, differ, but the process is similar. A two-year-old child vacillates (often from minute to minute) between being a negatively independent person who rejects advice and assistance from parents and other adults to being a frightened and dependent child wanting desperately to be comforted and protected.

The extremes in dependency and autonomy needs in trainees will not be as dramatic as with a child. In addition, because we are working with adults in the training process for counseling and psychotherapy, our students are considerably more socialized and will exert more control over their emotional responses to stressful situations (for example, counseling and supervision sessions). Nonetheless, we can expect the supervisee to want to perform as an independently functioning professional at certain times (generally when dealing with clients or other situations similar to those in which the trainee has experienced past successes), at other times the trainee appears quite similar to a Level 1 trainee who desires plenty of advice and specific directions from the supervisor. This trainee struggles to keep the gains that were made during the first stage and may react negatively to supervisors who suggest new ways of conceptualizing or intervening.

Motivation. The motivation of our trainee also changes. We left the Level 1 trainee at a point where confidence in certain basic skills and the ability to be helpful had reached a degree of consolidation. Exposure to more difficult clients and training in more complex theories and interventions shake this confidence in our Level 2 counselors. Consequently, motivation fluctuates as the individual's feelings of efficacy change due to successes and failures with clients. It is at this stage that some of our students go through real despair about ever becoming a therapist. Others distance themselves affectively, cognitively, or behaviorally from the therapy enterprise. This takes the form of forgetting tasks, becoming involved in research to the point of shortchanging practicum responsibilities, or deciding to become an "academic." Much of this behavior is due to the constant vacillation; the trainee who was discouraged or distant last week returns this week with high enthusiasm for clinical work.

Awareness. Awareness at Level 2 means that the trainee is free to focus more on the client and to empathize with the client's affect. This increased awareness is not necessarily a positive experience for the trainee. Becoming more aware of or empathizing more with the client can result in frustration for the trainee, as his or her conceptualization of the counseling process changes from a naive understanding to one of greater complexity.

Then, too, there are dangers in this increased focus on the client. The trainee may forge awareness of his or her own self and empathize with the client to the extent of being unable to provide effective interventions. This reaction, labeled countertransference by Peabody and Gelso (1982) and emotional contagion by Hoffman (1984), often leads counselors either to distance themselves from the client or, alternatively, to become enmeshed in the client's identity. Female trainees, due perhaps to a greater learned focus on relationships, may be especially vulnerable to this overidentification with the client. On the other hand, our clinical experience suggests that male trainees are more likely to emphasize gaining cognitive clarity over empathic understanding. In other words, females may tend to overaccommodate to the client's world, while males may retreat to tight constructs or assimilations. A task of this stage, then, is to gain an appropriate self-focus while maintaining focus on, and empathy for, the client.

One of our female doctoral students describes her experience in a way that incorporates much of what we have said about the Level 2 trainee:

> I was in my second practicum and was working with a suicidal client. I had worked with a mildly suicidal client before in my first practicum. When discussing my concern about the client with my (male) supervisor, he began listing the procedures I should go through if the client told me that he was going to commit suicide. At first I listened to the supervisor intently, but as the session went on I became more and more concerned about the client until I became so concerned that I could not even listen to the supervisor. He was still talking, but I was so upset I couldn't listen or think about what he was saying. My heart was racing and my stomach felt as if it was all tied up in knots. I wasn't concerned with what the supervisor would think of me if the client did commit suicide as I had been with my first suicidal client. Now I was concerned about the client and found myself imagining where the client might be and what the client might be doing at the moment. I remembered the client's feelings of hopelessness and felt this too. I said to myself, "Forget what the supervisor is saying. I will handle this the way I want to handle it." Yet, near the end of the session I had a question that seemed of major importance. I asked the supervisor and listened carefully as if the whole case rested on the supervisor's answer. I was motivated to help the client, thus, my concern about the possibility of suicide. Yet, when the situation was over I considered leaving counseling because I knew situations like this happen often in counseling and I didn't

know if I should survive another one. This situation was emotionally intense and I felt drained
after it was over.

Interaction of Structures and Domains

A trainee's progression through the levels for each domain is influenced by the training experiences provided in each
area, as well as the person's own idiosyncrasies. It is unlikely
that a given trainee will be at Level 2 for all of the domains at
any given point in time. Thus, it is important not to assume
that Level 2 performance in one area indicates a Level 2 stage
of development for all other areas.

Intervention Skills Competence. The Level 2 trainee is
increasingly comfortable with a greater array of intervention
skills, although these skills are not presently well integrated
with an overall theoretical orientation. A desire for learning
additional skills is noticeable, although direct demands by the
supervisor for learning specific skills may be met with resistance. An interesting phenomenon of Level 2 behavior is an
occasional decrement in one's ability to do therapy. In applying interventions, the new focus of this trainee on the client
(both cognitively and affectively) can actually hinder his or
her ability to counsel. The trainee no longer worries only about
accurately implementing an intervention but is now increasingly
focused on understanding the client. Thus, there may be more
confusion about what to do and less confidence in the effectiveness of whatever intervention is selected. An analogy from
the world of sports may be helpful. A young pitcher who has
primarily one pitch, say a fastball, will not be too concerned
about the appropriateness of using that pitch. A more developed pitcher with three or four pitches to choose from, and
with a more detailed understanding of the strengths and weaknesses of a given batter, may at times appear more confused and
less effective than the younger player. Given additional experience under the correct conditions, the second pitcher will again
surpass the first in his ability to get batters out.

Assessment Techniques. The trainee shows marked improvement in using diagnostic classifications (for example, DSM-III) but may not have a good sense of the ramifications of a particular classification for a given client. In other words, such classifications may suggest little to this trainee in terms of how the individual client interacts with her or his environment or what specific interventions should be implemented in therapy. As the trainee increasingly takes the client's perspective, diagnostic categories may appear rather cold, detached, and inimical to the sanctity of the individual. The trainee may lose interest in assessment techniques or resist using them. These methods no longer seem as useful in understanding the client as they appeared at Level 1.

Interpersonal Assessment. As mentioned previously, our trainee is now more aware of the client's perspective and affect in therapy. There is still considerable difficulty in separating useful responses to a client that are based on accurate perceptions of the client's interpersonal interactions from countertransference issues that are effectively blocked from awareness. In more behavioral terms, the trainee may be unaware of when he or she responds to a client based on his or her own idiosyncratic learning history and when the response is an accurate and objective assessment of cues emanating from the client. The counselor overaccommodates to the client's world view and often fails to utilize her or his own assimilative structures to see the whole picture.

Client Conceptualizations. Conceptualizations of the client are increasingly affected by a more accurate and complete understanding of the client's perspective. This can result either in more cogent and better articulated diagnoses or in a vague collection of exceptions to specific diagnostic classifications. The overaccommodation discussed above is again seen, as the counselor tends to view the client's world as the client sees it. Usually, obvious discrepancies between several parts of the client's story are overlooked and not integrated into the conceptualization. Often, conceptualizations by Level 2 trainees reflect the client's implicit theoretical orientation rather than the counselor's. Alternatively, an overassimilative approach ignores essential parts of the client's voice in the conceptualization.

Individual Differences. An increasing awareness of individual differences is incorporated in more complex client conceptualizations. Greater awareness of cultural and gender differences influences decisions regarding interventions and diagnosis. There is still, however, likely to be considerable stereotypical thinking done by the Level 2 trainee. For example, a supervisor can expect to periodically hear generalizations about how all females and all males respond to certain situations. Similarly, cultural guidelines for working with clients from various backgrounds may be applied with few adjustments made for the individual client.

On the other hand, the Level 2 trainee sometimes views the client as such a unique individual that basic information and theory on various types of individual differences are ignored. This specific client becomes the exception to every rule.

The domain of individual differences is one where often the most productive work at Level 2 is done. The trainee is now deeply aware of individual differences and, even if confused and vacillating, has greater openness to seeing and understanding the varieties of human experience.

Theoretical Orientation. Depending on the exposure to various theoretical orientations incorporated into the training program, Level 2 trainees often move away from allegiance to a specific theoretical orientation toward a more personalized, eclectic approach. If permitted by the supervisor, the trainee may use one orientation with some clients and other approaches with additional clients. In some cases, several different orientations and techniques may be used for a single case. What the trainee lacks at this point is an understanding of when to use which orientations or techniques. The trainee often has difficulty explaining why a particular orientation was used with a given client or justifying the choice and sequencing of techniques.

Treatment Goals and Plans. It is often more difficult for the Level 2 trainee to specify treatment goals and plans than it was for the Level 1 counselor. Overaccommodation to the client may result in despair about the probability of providing effective treatment. Confusion resulting from vague or conflicted conceptualizations often hinders the process of developing treatment plans. The Level 2 counselor is also particularly vulnerable to discouragement when initial treatment plans do not work.

Professional Ethics. Professional ethics are generally more easily understood by the Level 2 trainee than by the Level 1 trainee. At this level, the counselor begins to pay attention to the ramifications of ethical decisions for the client and may be more concerned with the role ethical behavior plays in protecting the client than in protecting the therapist. During the course of development at Level 2, the trainee gains an appreciation for the client's welfare. When the rights of more than one client are at stake, with possible negative consequences for one or both, the trainee is torn by allegiance to the clients and the necessity to behave ethically. For example, a trainee one of us recently worked with was in a therapeutic relationship with a man desiring help with controlling his anger. The trainee had gained an appreciation for this man's past experiences of being beaten by his father and ignored by his mother. The counselor had begun to understand this man's view of the world and to feel some of his pain and anger. During one session, the client reported that he had repeatedly struck his child the night before. The child had suffered some bruises but no permanent physical harm. The client felt awful and wanted the counselor to help him avoid such behavior in the future. The trainee was torn by his legal responsibility to inform child protective services of the incident and by his caring and empathy for his client.

Across the eight domains, supervision of the Level 2 trainee is more complicated and, perhaps, turbulent than supervision of the Level 1 trainee.

Empirical Evidence

Recent research on the supervision process has begun to focus on more experienced trainees. Evidence is accumulating that suggests that these counselors have different supervision needs than do their less experienced colleagues. We briefly examine this literature here. We want to note that little of the fluctuation and ambivalence we believe characteristic of Level 2 is evident from this research. The process described in these studies appears much more even and linear than we and our supervisees have experienced it. We will expand on this point later.

Reising and Daniels (1983) found differences between master's level and advanced master's level counselors in a number of areas. They reported that the more experienced group of counselors gained in self-perceived independence of action during counseling and supervision and were less anxious, less technique-oriented, and more ready for confrontation.

Similarly, Heppner and Roehlke (1984) (study 2) looked at perceptions of important supervisor behaviors across three trainee experience levels: beginning practicum, advanced practicum, and intern. The advanced practicum students (who we assume are roughly equivalent to Level 2 therapists) shared many responses with both beginning and intern level trainees. Certain supervisor behaviors were rated highly only by the advanced practicum students. Trainees at this level considered it important that the supervisor suggest alternative interventions and make direct suggestions when appropriate. These trainees also wanted the supervisor to make suggestions for alternative conceptualizations of the client. The selection of these behaviors indicates awareness of options in dealing with clients and the understanding that the trainee can benefit from such input by the supervisor. Other behaviors rated important by the advanced trainees were similarly rated by the beginning and intern level trainees.

In study 3, Heppner and Roehlke (1984) examined incidents in the supervision process reported by trainees as turning points in their developing effectiveness as counselors. Both beginning and advanced trainees (roughly one third of each) considered issues of competency as critical in their training. This reflects some dependency on the supervisor and the desire for approval. The most frequently noted category for advanced practicum students, however, revolved around issues of self-awareness. This category consisted of incidents concerning emotional awareness, confrontation, respect for individual differences, and personal motivation.

In a study examining supervisors' perceptions of their own behavior in supervision, Miars and others (1983) found supervisors tended to vary their approaches to supervision as a function of trainee experience level. For example, advanced practicum and intern level trainees were given less structure, direction, instruction, and support by the supervisors. More emphasis was placed on fostering personal development, tackling client resistance, and dealing with transference/countertransference issues with the more advanced trainees. These differences were more pronounced for psychoanalytically and psychodynamically oriented supervisors than for those who reported other orientations. This focus probably reflects a sensitivity to developmental issues characteristic of analytic/dynamic orientations to counseling and psychotherapy.

Other evidence is available from a longitudinal study by Hill, Charles, and Reed (1981). Twelve trainees in a counseling psychology program were followed through three years of training. Although it is impossible to be sure what stage these trainees had reached at the time of their exit interviews, it is safe to assume that some were Level 2 while others may have been entering Level 3. All of the trainees reported improved empathy for clients, while most reported that they were able to focus more on the client and less on their own performance. Behaviorally, these trainees saw themselves using more interpretation and confrontation with their clients, while being more relaxed, natural, less anxious, and more spontaneous. The trainees reported feeling at the beginning of their training that their supervisors knew everything, and they worried about the supervisors' judgments and evaluations. Over time, the trainee/supervisor relationship became more consultative as the trainees began to trust themselves more.

In an extensive study sampling eleven counseling agencies and 237 counselors, Worthington (1984) reported a trend for supervisors to encourage increasing independence in their trainees as they gained experience. Similar results were reported by McNeill, Stoltenberg, and Pierce (1985). They found significant differences between beginning and intermediate trainees on self-reported measures of increased self-awareness and desire for greater autonomy in counseling and supervision. A nonsignificant difference was noted on greater knowledge of theory and skills.

Taken together, these studies support the general thrust of Level 2 toward increased autonomy and awareness of self and others. The structure of motivation has not yet been explicitly explored. To us, Level 2 is the "clinician's stage"—one that is not clearly studied or supported in current research but that nevertheless is very real to those experiencing this stage's turmoil and to their supervisors. We have explored the existence of this stage with groups of advanced practicum students as well as with our own supervisees, and all acknowledge its reality. Several who assessed themselves as being at Level 2 said that it was a relief to hear that this was a normal, expected development. They believed that understanding the dimensions of Level 2 allowed them to "stick with it."

How do we explain the almost total absence of validation of Level 2 in research studies? It may be that we have not asked the right questions in the right way. Students on the other side (Level 3) may well discount or suppress the turmoil of the previous stage and see the process as more calm and linear than it really was. Our students, eager to be considered competent by themselves and others, report difficulty in acknowledging and discussing the ambivalence and pain of Level 2 even among themselves. Perhaps these issues are not always made salient for the trainee in supervision. A focus on therapy process in supervision might highlight these aspects and make them more amenable to resolution and integration.

The Supervision Environment

The supervision environment for the Level 2 trainee needs to be altered somewhat from that provided for our Level 1 supervisee. The Level 1 trainee needed considerable structure, specific instruction and training in various intervention techniques, and emphasis on increasing awareness. The Level 2 therapist is beginning to move on to other issues. Stoltenberg (1981) describes the appropriate supervision environment for this individual as highly autonomous, with little structure imposed by the supervisor. The supervisor should support, clarify ambivalence, provide modeling, and use less of a didactic focus. At the same time, the supervisor must be prepared to modify this environment in response to issues of client welfare. The supervisor must remember that the supervisee at this stage only knows that something is wrong and as yet lacks the tools to fix it. This trainee, when disappointed and angry, may also be disappointed and angry with the supervisor. The supervisor is then viewed as "an incompetent or inadequate figure who has failed to come through when he or she was so badly needed" (Loganbill, Hardy, and Delworth, 1982, p. 19).

Client Assignment. Let us first examine the assignment of clients to trainees. The Level 1 counselor was usually assigned reasonably well functioning clients so that the trainee would not be overwhelmed with pathology and could focus on learning and applying basic counseling skills. At one of our training sites, we often introduce our beginning trainees to the counseling process by assigning them fairly straightforward, vocationally indecisive clients who are functioning well in other areas of their lives. The more advanced Level 2 trainees, however, are more likely to see depressed, anxious, or acting out clients who are less amenable to change via simple structured approaches. We may also begin work in relationship and family counseling with Level 2 trainees. This increased population of presenting problems can be exciting and challenging for the trainee but may also induce frustration and anxiety as previous effective counselor behavior proves less than sufficient in dealing with more complex problems.

The supervisor needs to provide a blend of clients for the Level 2 trainee. There should be a percentage of clients who are relatively well functioning with whom the trainee can consolidate previously learned counseling behaviors. In addition, a few difficult clients should be assigned in order to challenge the trainee's ability to respond flexibly to new problems. It is very important to monitor the trainee's progress on an ongoing basis with all clients during this stage. Performance in counseling is likely to result in uneven success across clients. It is during this stage of development that the supervisee is likely to engage in the most pronounced resistance toward the supervisor. We have suggested a highly autonomous environment for this trainee; use of this new freedom by the trainee can be indicative of his or her stage of development.

The supervisor can learn much by noticing which clients the trainee chooses to focus on during supervision sessions. Due to trainee ambivalence toward autonomy, we are likely to find the trainee wanting to discuss clients with whom he or she feels successful. We periodically have our supervisee come to supervision apparently completely baffled by a client and desiring us to provide a conceptualization and interventions for the trainee to try in the next session. We are less likely to see the trainee want to discuss a client with whom he or she feels vaguely uncertain or somehow stuck. In addition, some of the clients with whom our trainee becomes impatient or angry may be the most important for us to focus on in supervision. With such clients, the opportunity exists to help the trainee identify therapeutic blocks or countertransference issues that can frustrate growth. The trainee's growing desire for independence, however, may limit his or her awareness of what is fruitful to pursue in supervision. As previously noted, it is very important at this stage to support independence in our trainees and encourage risk taking with clients. It is also important to be sensitive to the trainee's uncertainty regarding competence and fear of negative evaluation by the supervisor. It is inappropriate at this stage to allow the trainee a completely free hand in working with clients. It is equally important, however, to be careful in how we protect clients and still encourage growth in the trainee. The skill required to provide a good deal of autonomy yet still be watchful is one of the most difficult in the art of supervision!

Supervisor Interventions. Loganbill, Hardy, and Delworth (1982) described five categories of intervention: facilitative, confrontive, conceptual, prescriptive, and catalytic. We argue that facilitative or supportive interventions should serve as the basis for the supervisor/trainee relationship at all stages. Recent research in supervision supports the importance of a supportive environment by trainees across experience levels (for example, Rabinowitz, Heppner, and Roehlke, 1985). It is no less important for the Level 2 trainee than for others. A supportive environment allows the trainee the freedom to deal with anxiety-provoking or threatening issues without fear of unfair or personal attacks by the supervisor.

Prescriptive interventions—when the supervisor makes specific suggestions or demands for a particular intervention or treatment approach—most likely occur with Level 1 trainees. Although such interventions may be necessary to protect client welfare or to encourage the trainee to try new techniques, over-reliance on this approach most likely induces reactance or resistance and may limit growth by reducing the conflict produced by uncertainty in working with a client. We want to encourage this trainee to integrate his or her personal attributes with a counseling orientation, and we may stunt such growth if we require the trainee to do what we would do in working with a given client. This may be frustrating for the supervisor (much like watching your child make mistakes or take a tumble when you know you could prevent it), but learning through error can be as facilitative as learning through success. The trainee's right to experiment and fail (given protection of client welfare) must be respected.

The increasing focus of the Level 2 trainee on the client results in him or her interacting with the client on a more intimate basis. As noted above, this can result in countertransference on the part of the trainee or susceptibility to overt or covert client manipulations. Process comments by the supervisor can bring these dynamics to awareness and help the trainee more effectively use the additional information about the client (and him- or herself) now available. These process comments are similar in spirit to what Loganbill, Hardy, and Delworth (1982) call catalytic interventions. They tend to "stir things up" and bring processes to the trainee's awareness that would otherwise go unnoticed.

Conceptual interventions are particularly useful for the Level 2 trainee. Loganbill, Hardy, and Delworth (1982, p. 33) describe these interventions as "offering substantive content in the form of theories and principles to the benefit of the supervisee." Alternative ways to conceptualize a client or the treatment process are helpful for this trainee as she or he strives to learn about therapy and integrate this knowledge with personal attributes. To our knowledge, no one personality theory or approach to counseling and psychotherapy has yet been proven to be most accurate or effective. It is imperative, then, that the trainee be exposed to more than one orientation so that the most useful theory (or combination of theories) and techniques can be adopted by the trainee. The supervisor should offer alternative conceptualizations and encourage the trainee to view events from a number of perspectives. As all supervisors cannot work comfortably within all theoretical orientations, the Level 2 trainee should be exposed to supervisors adhering to differing approaches to therapy.

It is important to realize that just because something is good for a trainee does not mean that the trainee will be in favor of it. Recently, a couple of our students were assigned to a supervisor who adhered to an orientation markedly different from the ones to which the students had primarily been exposed. These two trainees had developed considerable skills in cognitive-behavioral techniques and were comfortable conceptualizing the counseling process in those terms. Considerable resistance occurred when these students began supervision with an analytically oriented therapist. This supervisor's use of analytic concepts and focus on parallel processes in supervision and counseling created considerable anxiety and attacking behavior on the part of the trainees. They felt that they were being forced to abandon what had been working well for them in favor of a system that fit the supervisor's needs and not their own. The supervisor, on the other hand, felt that the trainees were overly resistant and questioned their defensiveness and unwillingness to alter the way they worked with clients.

We suspect that both parties were partially correct in their evaluation of the situation. In our opinion, it is unfair for a supervisor to demand that trainees completely abandon what they are comfortable with in counseling because he or she favors an alternative approach. On the other hand, it is also inappropriate for trainees to refuse to entertain other perspectives on the counseling process. We suggest that conceptual interventions occur within a safe environment in order to expand the theoretical and technical horizons of our students. Especially with the Level 2 trainee, considerably more progress occurs if persuasive as opposed to punitive approaches are used to encourage growth.

Conceptual interventions also aid the trainee in the essential process of balancing accommodation to the world of the client with building more sturdy and useful assimilations, or cognitive structures. For our overaccommodative trainees, conceptual interventions can directly aid in helping the counselor use information from the client but assimilate it into his or her own framework. For overassimilators, these interventions help the counselor gain understanding (accommodation) of the client's view. In both cases, the end product is expanded assimilations, which are then available to the counselor for further work in the accommodation/assimilation process.

We have suggested that a supportive and structured environment is best suited for Level 1 trainees. Confrontive interventions for these trainees is too threatening to them to allow for evaluation and integration of whatever insight is being suggested by the supervisor. This is no longer the case with Level 2 trainees. Although a supportive environment is necessary for a confrontive intervention to have its greatest impact, the counselor "ego strength" should be sufficient to allow the supervisor to bring discrepancies to the trainee's awareness. Loganbill, Hardy, and Delworth (1982) note that such discrepancies or inconsistencies can occur in the supervisee's feelings and emotions, attitudes and beliefs, and behaviors and actions. Identifying these problems creates dissonance within the individual, which stimulates attempts at integration and reequilibration.

Interactional styles of supervisors affect the manner in which confrontation occurs. Generally, we suggest that the supervisor be careful to convey acceptance of the supervisee as a person and a counselor-in-training. In our experience, very powerful confrontations can be presented to the trainee in a low-key, matter-of-fact way. The content of the confrontation is sufficient to produce internal conflict in the supervisee; it is not necessary to underline the importance of the confrontation by aggressive, punitive, or superior behavior on the part of the supervisor. For example, one of us recently pointed out to a male supervisee that he appeared much more timid and deferential with a middle-aged female client than he did with any of his other clients. His response was one of surprise and confusion, but the casual way the discrepancy was introduced reduced the possibility of defensiveness on his part. By the next supervision session, the trainee had realized that his upbringing prescribing courteous behavior toward older women was limiting his freedom to address important issues with his client.

Supervisees have different learning styles and thresholds of anxiety. For some, merely pointing out discrepancies in an "isn't it interesting" or "have you noticed that" approach will be sufficient. Their own motivation and trust in you is sufficient for them to effortfully consider your feedback. Other, perhaps less sensitive, trainees need more forceful confrontations to produce the conflict necessary to stimulate growth.

Social Psychological Influence. The interpersonal influence process introduced in Chapter Three provides additional guidance on how to affect a supervisee's attitudes and encourage exploration and growth. As noted earlier, the Elaboration Likelihood Model of persuasion (Petty and Cacioppo, 1981) describes the interactive effects of various factors in a persuasion setting (which is certainly characteristic of supervision). We noted that Level 1 trainees are the most susceptible to the influence of the supervisor as an authority figure. The Level 2 trainee is less inclined to take the supervisor's word for something without critically evaluating its merits using some internal set of criteria or by comparing it to advice from other "experts." This resistance to the demands of authority figures can be frustrating for the supervisor who prefers obedience and subservience on the part of supervisees. For the secure supervisor, however, this presents a challenge and a true opportunity to promote growth in the trainee.

Social psychological research tells us that the more one

knows (or thinks she or he knows) about a given topic, the less susceptible one is to persuasive attempts. We also know that increased knowledge can result in greater efforts to evaluate alternative options or conceptualizations of an issue. Simply put, it is easier to produce attitude change—and subsequent behavioral change—in someone if that individual knows a bit about the issue. The Level 2 trainee has learned a lot about clients and the counseling process. He or she is less likely to take a supervisor's advice without an accompanying convincing rationale. This provides the supervisor with an opportunity to encourage central route processing (effortful consideration of an issue) on the part of the trainee. The result of such a process should be a better understanding of the issue at hand, which should then affect the supervisee's behavior in counseling and in supervision.

An example may be helpful here. During a supervision session with a beginning trainee, one of the authors noted that the supervisee had become stuck in working with his client and stopped the videotape to consider what was happening. The trainee was at a loss concerning what to do, so the supervisor suggested an intervention also appropriate for future similar situations. The trainee dutifully wrote down exactly what the supervisor said, and during a later session, that precise wording was heard on the videotape. A similar situation occurred with the same supervisor with a Level 2 trainee. In this case, the trainee initially downplayed the importance of the interaction on the videotape by insisting that he had already decided how to handle similar situations in the future. At that point, he noted some other work on the tape that he wanted to focus upon. In a nonthreatening manner, the supervisor suggested that it might be helpful for their work together if the supervisor knew how the trainee intended to deal with similar situations down the road. The trainee then described an intervention that the supervisor felt did not have much potential for avoiding similar difficulties in the future. Rather than attack the trainee's conceptualization of the problem, though, the supervisor showed interest in learning what the trainee perceived as later ramifications of that intervention and asked to be enlightened regarding the theoretical and empirical bases for such a decision. The trainee's explanation led to what appeared to the supervisor as a creative (though probably inaccurate) conclusion. The supervisor then offered an alternative suggestion, with accompanying rationale, for the trainee to consider. A week later, to the supervisor's surprise, the trainee implemented a variation of the suggested intervention with favorable results.

The process that occurred above, we believe, is central route processing by the advanced trainee and peripheral route processing by the beginning trainee. While the beginner was able only to mimic the supervisor, the advanced trainee was capable of integrating the concepts and the behavior. By pursuing the rationale provided by the trainee for his course of action (actually, encouraging the rationale to be produced), the supervisor forced the trainee into self-evaluation. Subsequently, when an alternative intervention was proposed (within a supportive environment), the trainee was able to evaluate the suggestion without becoming resistant to being told what to do. The primary responsibilities of the supervisor in such situations are attempting to listen to and understand the trainee, providing a supportive environment, and being able to produce a cogent rationale for suggestions concerning the trainee's conceptualization of the process and therapeutic behaviors.

Recent research on the Elaboration Likelihood Model (ELM) suggests the importance of emotions in persuasion and information processing. Bratt and Stoltenberg (1987) have found that central route processing (that is, careful, effortful thinking) is more likely to occur when the person's current mood is congruent with the mood felt by the person during a particular situation. For example, if a trainee experiences depression or dysphoria when working with a client in a session, the supervisor should encourage the trainee to reexperience that affect when discussing the client in supervision. This allows the trainee more ready access to schema-related information that may be important in considering alternatives. In short, different information is more easily accessible to the trainee when he or she experiences different moods. Tapping the more congruent mood can facilitate working through the process. (See Stoltenberg and McNeill (1987) for a more detailed discussion.)

The Elaboration Likelihood Model also warns us about biased processing. Just because trainees invest a considerable amount of cognitive effort in evaluating alternatives does not mean that they approach the task with open minds. We can encourage such openness on the part of the trainees by being open toward their ideas. We can also use effective confrontation as a mechanism for encouraging self-evaluation. Appropriately used, confrontation can cut through much of the biased processing done by our trainees and open the door for growth to higher levels of development.

Caveats and Transitions

Much of the above material implies that supervision of a Level 2 trainee proceeds as smoothly as it often does with a Level 1 (or Level 3) supervisee. Nothing is further from the truth. The fluctuation, ambivalence, and confusion present at Level 2 simply do not permit the week-to-week development generally seen in Levels 1 and 3. One of our students, classifying herself at Level 2 during an advanced practicum, noted that "it feels like adolescence all over again. I'd like the clarity of childhood back, even though I know it's too simplistic. And I know I just have to keep working on it until I reach adulthood." We have found that sharing this model, especially Level 2, with students is helpful for them. Knowledge of the model "normalizes" their struggle and gives them a useful conceptual blueprint.

We have stated that cognitive interventions are generally most productive for Level 2 trainees, allowing them to regain some stability and move forward to Level 3. Our clinical experience, plus reports from students, suggest that this may be more true for female supervisees. Just as we hypothesize that a woman's generally stronger affect may cause her to become enmeshed in the client's world, her tolerance for affect may allow her to wallow too long in the confusion and ambivalence of Level 2. Cognitive interventions, appropriately applied, can assist her toward the integration and stability characteristic of Level 3.

On the other hand, males, finding the affective distress intolerable, may tend toward premature closure on Level 2. The danger for women is that they may wallow too long; for men the danger may be that they will circumvent the process by striving for cognitive clarity without empathic understanding and move on to a pseudo Level 3 without real change. It is essential to provide for some of our male trainees support and affective interventions that will allow them to tolerate appropriate ambivalence and confusion before moving on.

The distinction between providing supervision and providing psychotherapy is most often an issue with Level 2 trainees. Issues of overidentification with the client or countertransference are frequent. Usually these can be dealt with in the supervision session, as noted earlier in the case of the young male trainee and the older woman client. However, when these issues with clients are both pervasive and persistent, the question of psychotherapy for the trainee is relevant. Our experience is that most trainees appreciate the supervisor raising this issue in a supportive manner and, if indicated, facilitating the trainee entering therapy with an appropriate professional.

It is vital that the supervisor of a Level 2 trainee maintain flexibility (and hopefully a sense of humor) during this confusing and "adolescent" stage. These may well be the most difficult trainees to supervise, but they can be highly rewarding as well. Probably they are not the best group with which to begin a supervisory career and are better assigned to experienced supervisors who can tolerate the ambivalence. For such supervisors, there is great joy in seeing their confused students move into the calmer waters of Level 3 with a new and deeper sense of confidence and competence.

As fluctuations decrease, the transition to Level 3 begins. Level 3 is characterized by more affective calm and a great deal of concerted work on the part of both supervisor and supervisee to consolidate prior skills and add new ones. If the trainee moves into this level near the end of training, with the world of active professional work near, there can be a hurried flavor to the supervisory work. If Level 1 is characterized as a short series of vertical lines, as the trainee learns a bit in many domains, and Level 2 as a jagged sequence of lines representing mountains and valleys, Level 3 looks more like a horizontal line with several vertical ones intersecting it. This represents the essential task of this level—to move across domains and to add appropriate knowledge and skill.

6

Developmental Level Three:

Challenge and Growth

Level 3 is best summarized as "the calm after the storm." The trainee is relatively free of the fluctuations typical of Level 2 and is able to concentrate on development within and across domains. For most trainees, this level is a critical point in the process of becoming a therapist. Increased stability at the structural level allows for freedom to concentrate on each domain and often facilitates rapid development. Although, as noted previously, the levels are only roughly commensurate with experience, many predoctoral interns (especially in the last part of the internship) and new doctoral level professionals are best described by Level 3 structures, at least in certain domains.

Level 3 Integrated represents for us an integration of Level 3 structures across domains, that is, the professional is able to demonstrate development of Level 3 structures across the essential domains and is steadily moving to deeper awareness. While further learning remains a life-long practice, the Level 3 Integrated therapist is considered a "master therapist" by many and is often sought as a supervisor by younger trainees.

Level 3 Structures

Stoltenberg (1981) speaks of an increased sense of personal counselor identity and professional self-confidence at

Level 3. The supervisee is becoming "a counselor who is characterized by an increased empathy toward others and a more highly differentiated interpersonal orientation" (p. 63).

Motivation. The motivation of this trainee is more stable. Doubts regarding the profession may well remain, however. The difference seems to be that the doubts are not disabling, and the supervisee is able to live with "commitment in the face of doubt" (Reising and Daniels, 1983, p. 241). Thus, the day-to-day motivation of this trainee is relatively consistent. The supervisee is focused on becoming a competent professional and does not allow doubts or questions to interfere with this process. Because trainees often arrive at this level when they are making decisions regarding other professional roles, where they wish to seek employment, and other personal decisions, issues of motivation are typically discussed in supervision. The issue is how the counselor/therapist role will fit into the trainee's total professional and personal identity. The trainee often wants to explore more deeply her or his motivations toward becoming a therapist. The relative calm and freedom of this level in terms of both affect and cognition allow a more insightful look at trainee motivations without disrupting basic commitment and behavior regarding psychotherapy.

Loganbill, Hardy, and Delworth (1982) provide a useful discussion of six general areas of motivating factors that bring trainees into the profession and that can be usefully sorted at Level 3. The factors are intimacy, power, financial concerns, personal growth, intellectual abilities, and altruism. In their view, each motivating factor has both positive and negative aspects. The Level 3 trainee is able to become aware of his or her unique constellation of motivations and to channel them constructively in working with clients. Unhealthy motivations are brought to awareness and consciously controlled by the trainee. The supervisor can serve as a supportive friend in this process, helping reality test the trainee's perceptions and sharing similar experiences.

Autonomy. Trainees at Level 3 have a firm belief in their own autonomy that is not easily threatened. This sense allows the trainee to be dependent on the supervisor in appropriate situations, such as those necessary for further development in one or more domains. For the most part, the supervisee carries out clinical activities in a fairly autonomous manner. He or she no longer tends to be a "staunch and unvarying disciple of any given technique" (Stoltenberg, 1981, p. 63). Supervisees at this level also demonstrate increased tolerance for colleagues who hold different theoretical positions or who endorse different treatment techniques. In fact, they may seek out such individuals as supervisors. "At this point," stated one intern trainee, "I know who I am and need a supervisor who will respect that and help me with things I still need to learn."

Self- and Other-Awareness. The shift here is the most dramatic in the three structures, and fosters change in the other two. Our trainees are now basically accepting of self, which reflects an insightful awareness of both strengths and weaknesses. They are not unduly frightened by, nor defensive about, the weaker areas. They have confidence that they can grow in these areas. Empathy is increased to the point where the counselor can be with the client but can also pull back and process her or his own feelings and thoughts. Where the Level 2 trainee might lose him- or herself in the client's experiencing, the Level 3 therapist is able to focus intently on the client, empathetically understand his or her world, and still pull back and objectively process information—including his or her own reactions. The supervisee can also be aware of the supervisor's affect and cognition and be unafraid to deal with these. It is not unusual for Level 3 trainees to provide significant support to their supervisors as the supervisors go through periods of professional or personal stress.

The increased self- and other-awareness characteristic of the Level 3 therapist allows for more complete use of the therapist's self in sessions. It also enables the trainee to access useful theoretical and technical information while interacting with a client in a session. Thus, the therapist now has access to important information from the client, valuable personal, emotional, and cognitive responses to the client, and theoretical and empirical background developed in training to date.

This increased awareness aids supervisees in determining the role of therapy in their professional career. Counseling is seen more realistically for what it is, and the match between this activity and the trainee is looked at closely. Some choose to make the therapist role a central one; others do not. One intern put it this way: "It's great to know that I can do therapy, and I want to continue growing in this area. But research really turns me on more, and I like teaching, too. Given who I am, I think I'd like an academic role best."

Interaction of Structures and Domains

Our generally autonomous Level 3 supervisee is largely aware of his or her strengths and weaknesses within and across domains. The supervisee now has the affective and cognitive energy to tackle weaknesses and to accept setbacks in the process. It is quite likely that the confusion and fluctuation of Level 2 will persist in one or more domains, especially as the supervisee makes the transition to Level 3.

As supervisees make this transition, it is important for them and their supervisors to assess competency across domains. Special attention needs to be directed toward those domains in which the trainee continues to function with Level 2 characteristics. However, this attention should not deter development in other areas. In fact, more advanced work can initiate a powerful push in other domains that allows trainees to leave the lower level structures behind.

It is common for Level 3 supervisees to revert briefly when faced with a new task. One of us recalls a solid Level 3 trainee who reverted to inconsistent motivation, confusion, and dependency when faced with the task of conceptualizing a couple rather than an individual. With minimum, well-focused supervisory input, the trainee was able to "talk herself" back to Level 3 within one session. At that point, we brought up the domain issue of assessment, and she was able to ask for assistance.

Intervention Skills Competence. Our trainees at this level are experienced with quite a number of interventions. The task

here is to better integrate interventions with client conceptualizations and treatment plans and to increase the trainees' ability
to make changes in interventions during the counseling session.
This is an important task for most trainees moving into Level 3
and one on which the majority make steady and sure progress.
For some trainees, this becomes a time to learn new and unfamiliar intervention methods as well. For example, a number of
our trainees at this level seek training in use of clinical hypnosis.
One of our postdoctoral supervisees, who held a generally dynamic orientation, discovered a need to learn more about some
basic cognitive and behavioral techniques. Another discovered a
need to read more on college student development as he entered
a university counseling center setting.

Typically, trainees at this level are more creative in their
use of interventions. They experiment more, based on confidence in their ability to "switch tracks" if one type of intervention is not effective with the client.

Assessment Techniques. The trainee has moved from
overreliance on these techniques in Level 1 through a questioning, often negative stance in Level 2. At Level 3, the supervisee
develops a solid sense of the role of assessment techniques in
her or his work and also develops clear preferences for specific
techniques. Those techniques that seem appropriate to the
counselor's work are learned well and used frequently. As with
intervention skills, a number of supervisees seek training on
techniques and instruments with which they have little familiar-
ity. In our experience, this domain is often more influenced by
setting than others because settings differ a great deal in the
attention paid to various techniques. If the trainee moves into
Level 3 at the start of internship, for example, his or her focus
in this domain will be heavily influenced by the internship setting. Trainees who enter Level 3 earlier have a tendency to evaluate internship settings in terms of how the assessment philosophy of the setting fits with that of the trainee.

Interpersonal Assessment. Level 3 trainees move away
from stereotypical thinking. While models and general informa-

tion are still of value, the counselor focuses primarily on the client and his or her own reactions to the client. The counselor sees each client as a unique individual and relies less on pigeon-holing the client on the basis of such variables as age, gender, or (especially) diagnostic category. The trainee develops an in-creased sense of how such variables influence the client's life and how they can be sources of strength as well as psycho-pathology. At this level, the supervisee's understanding of the client is often fuller than that of the supervisor, who has not generally interacted with the client.

The twin processes of accommodation and assimilation operate more in unison at this level, although not without some struggle. This domain, more than any other, is characterized by appropriate awareness of both self and other. Parallel processes between counselor/client and counselor/supervisor dyads are more frequent, explicit, and usefully worked with now.

Client Conceptualizations. Increasingly, changed aware-ness of self and others allows conceptualizations of clients that are neither overaccommodative or overassimilative. As in the domain of interpersonal assessment, the trainee is now aware of how client variables interact to produce the whole person. A conceptualization for one client is different from that for an-other, even if the two carry the same diagnostic label. The trainee is now able to label the client diagnostically, while at the same time focusing on patterns relevant for this client as an individual.

Individual Differences. The shift away from stereotypical thinking allows the supervisee to build productively on good work accomplished at Level 2. Trainees typically continue their interest in cultural and other differences and are now able to more effectively view clients as both individuals and "persons in context." If the counselor is working with a new client popula-tion, she or he will be especially motivated to learn as much as possible about this group.

Theoretical Orientation. The trainee's theoretical orienta-tion, unfrozen at Level 2, firms up again at this more knowledgeable and flexible state. The Level 3 trainee does adhere to a particular theoretical orientation, but now he or she uses this perspective rather than being driven by the theory. This trainee tends not to be threatened by a supervisor who holds a differing orientation but generally values and enjoys the dialogue about different theoretical views. The orientation is used in assessment and intervention work with the client but never with the rigidity of Level 1.

Treatment Goals and Plans. Appropriate learning across domains produces a cyclical flow among the assessment/conceptualization/intervention phases of therapy. When this process breaks down, it is often due to a lack of competency in one of the relevant domains. Most often, this is recognized by both supervisor and supervisee and is appropriately addressed. Treatment plans are a key linchpin in holding this whole process together. We see Level 3 as the time when trainees are finally ready to make real progress in this domain. As they grow and stabilize in their ability to work with the first six domains, treatment plans begin to flow from assessment and conceptualization and are appropriately altered as a result of interventions. Plans become more focused and coherent, and trainees learn to fine-tune them as therapy progresses.

Professional Ethics. Level 3 trainees have a broadened perspective on ethical issues. They expect—rather than are confused by—the reality that different principles of their professional code seem to contradict each other. They seek out and use knowledge of broader ethical guidelines in addressing ethical dilemmas. They are able to handle very complex issues. For instance, trainees at this level can integrate both the prohibition against sexual activity with clients and the reality of sexual attraction toward specific clients. There is less need to suppress these feelings in order to adhere to the injunctions of the ethical code.

In addition, supervisees become aware of codes beyond their profession. Some of these apply to specific work settings and specific activities. For example, interns in a counseling center learn and integrate the codes of the American College Personnel Association (ACPA) and the National Association of Student Personnel Administrators (NASPA), along with the more familiar code of the American Psychological Association (APA). Many times, these codes address different issues—often administrative in nature—and help the supervisee to gain a broader picture of the context of counseling work.

Additional Considerations. Differences of gender or ethnicity appear to play a less compelling role with Level 3 trainees but only if previous tasks have been negotiated successfully. The danger for some women continues to be regression to the confusion and affective fluctuation characteristic of Level 2. There may also be some gender-linked problems in becoming autonomous in clinical work if trainees have not established appropriate autonomy in other aspects of their lives.

For some males, the danger of partial attainment of Level 3 structures continues to be present. One of us recalls an intern level male supervisee whose verbal sophistication and solid competencies disguised his lack of awareness of both self and client as well as a low level of motivation regarding his own development. He was stuck in a confusion which frightened him, but until he resolved these issues, no further development was possible.

For members of ethnic minorities who have not achieved an integration of their ethnic culture with the culture of counseling, the diffuse anger of Level 2 is likely to persist. This interferes to some degree with full achievement of Level 3 autonomy, motivation, and awareness. It is only the supervisee able to move comfortably in both cultures who can master the competencies necessary across domains. As one trainee, moving into Level 3, stated, "It has to be okay to be both a Chicano and a psychologist, or it's not worth going on." (See Chapter Ten for further discussion of this topic.)

For most professionals, the work of Level 3 persists until the end of formal supervision and often beyond. Our observation is that the majority of counselors function as solid Level 3 therapists. They work with reasonably consistent motivation, autonomy, and self-awareness. They are competent in each domain and have achieved some reasonable integration across domains. They are ourselves and most of our colleagues.

Some therapists, however, seem to go further, to achieve some qualities and expertise that cause others to recognize them as "master therapists." It is this development we have termed Level 3 Integrated.

Level 3 Integrated

Structures do not change at Level 3 Integrated. Instead, this additive level is characterized by a more complete and complex integration across domains. This integration adds fullness and richness to clinical work by allowing the counselor to move easily and efficiently from one domain to the other, using competencies gained in one to enhance the other. Clinical work develops a rhythm, with the counselor focusing on issues of assessment, then intervention, then recycling in more complex ways. Structural changes do not typically occur with these therapists, although traumatic life events can cause temporary regression in one or more areas. Rather, it is the broadening of knowledge and clinical experiences that allow this therapist to use him or herself to the fullest. It is the ease of this integration and recycling that prompts others to call Level 3 Integrated counselors "master therapists." The experience here is one of continued horizontal development that explores each domain in increasing depth and complexity.

In our experience, it is extremely rare for supervisees to reach this level by the end of the predoctoral internship. The modal time required appears to be five or six years of professional experience. Of course, the majority of us probably do not make this integration and continue to work at the linearly advanced but less horizontally integrated Level 3. What makes the difference? Our impression is that doing full-time, or nearly full-time, clinical work while at Level 3 helps. Also, supervision by someone who has attained Level 3 Integrated provides very useful modeling. Several of our colleagues state that working as supervisors aids themselves in this process. As one of them put it, "When I'm supervising, I'm forced to be articulate and clear about connections across domains, and that makes it easier for me to integrate." Finally, advanced levels in conceptual, ego, and moral development appear to be prerequisites for Level 3 Integrated.

On occasion, we have been surprised to see a reliable, solid Level 3 therapist add the integrative element of Level 3 Integrated after many years of practice. Our sense is that transitions and growth in personal life trigger this development in the professional arena. One colleague, after some years of teaching, doing research, and raising two children as a single parent, recycled into a clinical career and clearly achieved Level 3 Integrated in a short time. "Raising the kids and going through a lot of personal stresses just gave me a deeper and more rapid understanding of how everything fits together for and about clients" was his explanation.

Level 3 Integrated is our own construct, built on Hogan's (1964) and Stoltenberg's (1981) Level Four. This construct has not been subjected to empirical scrutiny as yet. To us and our counseling colleagues, its existence is proven by the presence among us of those who have become more than Level 3 and who represent something of excellence in the field of counseling and psychotherapy.

Empirical Evidence

Empirical evidence, as we have seen in Chapters Four and Five, supports the idea of differing needs and perceptions in supervisees over time. In a number of studies (for example, Hill, Charles, and Reed, 1981; Heppner and Roehlke, 1984; Worthington, 1984; Reising and Daniels, 1983; McNeill, Stoltenberg, and Pierce, 1985), trainees are shown to move from initial levels of anxiety and dependence to increased self-awareness and autonomy. Reising and Daniels (1983) report a particularly interesting result concerning motivation in postdoctoral professionals. These counselors experience persistent doubts regarding both the helpfulness of counseling and their own therapeutic skill but also indicate a continuing commitment to the profession. It may be, note Reising and Daniels (1983, p. 241), that these counselors are "more able to live with these doubts because of their deepened self-awareness and appropriately adjusted expectations about the profession."

There are problems with this research. We do not know the developmental level of supervisees in these studies. Also most studies include few, if any, trainees who might be expected to be functioning at Level 3, that is, interns and postdegree professionals. Nevertheless, the directions we hypothesize appear supported. More advanced supervisees in these studies are characterized by increased awareness, consistent motivation (in the face of doubt), and both desire and need for greater autonomy.

The Supervisory Environment

If patience is the hallmark of the supervisor of a Level 1 trainee and flexibility the requirement for Level 2, wisdom is the focus for those who provide supervision to Level 3 counselors. On the surface, the task appears fairly easy. After all, these supervisees are more aware, committed, and motivated. And they are more able to go about their work in an autonomous manner. Why is wisdom called for? Let us look at some of the difficulties.

First, the supervisee may be a "pseudo 3," that is, the supervisee described in Chapter Five who escaped the turmoil of Level 2 by pretending to have it all together and, in many cases, believing this to be the case. While firmly planted in the rigid and dualistic ground of Level 1, the supervisee achieved a more sophisticated way of articulating client concerns and the process of therapy. Such trainees are hard to assess, especially if they are at a more advanced level of training (for example, intern or postdegree) where Level 3 might be considered the norm.

In addition, few supervisees have attained Level 3 across domains and thus may perplex and surprise the supervisor. The supervisee whose intervention plan seems carefully thought-out and who appears aware of both client and self can rapidly appear the confused Level 2 trainee when asked to conceptualize the client.

With the fully developed Level 3, the challenge is to provide sufficient stimulation and challenge to lay the groundwork for the additive integration of Level 3 Integrated. And this prospect can arouse anxiety in the less experienced or less confident supervisor.

So, wisdom is called for. The appropriate supervisory environment for the Level 3 trainee is both flexible and person-oriented. The supervisor must be able to engage the supervisee in a careful and honest assessment of strengths and weaknesses across domains. The supervisor must assess the amount and type of awareness of self and client the supervisee possesses, the solidity of the supervisee's motivation, and her or his ability to function in an autonomous manner. Supervisees at this level have the most unique and idiosyncratic patterns of development and competencies. An effective supervisory environment requires a supervisor who can form and maintain a working alliance with the supervisee in order to explore and affect these patterns. Such an alliance provides a foundation the supervisor can use to push the trainee toward integration across domains.

The supervisor should be comfortable with and skilled at the use of confrontation while maintaining a supportive stance. It is essential to confront the supervisee with discrepancies between his or her functioning at a given moment and his or her more consistent level of functioning. It is also necessary to confront pseudo Level 3 development, discrepancies in competencies, and lack of integration across domains.

Wisdom is needed to know both how and when to confront. For example, it may not be immediately apparent to a supervisor why a usually effective counselor is having difficulties with a particular client. In most cases, it is also not apparent to the supervisee. The supervisor must be careful to avoid simple transmission of information regarding the client. Time must be taken for a joint exploration of the situation. Often, the result of such interaction is identification of either a deficit in one of the domains that was unknown to the supervisee and supervisor or an issue or bias that interferes with understanding and communicating with the client. Support, exploration, and confrontation may all be necessary to resolve situations such as this.

Supervision of a Level 3 counselor requires a supervisor who is functioning at the same level. In a situation where supervisees are free to choose supervisors, Level 3 supervisees often choose someone at the same level. Matched with a supervisor functioning below Level 3, the supervisee usually experiences a temporary and slight decline in motivation, autonomy, and awareness. This is especially true when the supervisor offers an intrusive and highly structured environment. In response, the Level 3 supervisee often appears dependent, minimally motivated, and closed off to self-awareness. In other words, the supervisee begins to look more like Level 2 trainees. Some supervisees survive such an environment through "game playing" and "giving supervisors what they want," while behaving at their own developmental level in contacts with clients, trainees, and colleagues.

Less damage results when an ambiguous supervisory environment is offered to the Level 3 supervisee by a less developed supervisor. Without an intrusive assault the supervisee makes a minimal accommodation to the supervisor and maintains his or her original level of functioning. Not much happens—opportunities for growth are lost—but the supervisee survives intact. In both of the above situations, the Level 3 therapist may seek out informal supervision from an advanced therapist in an attempt to compensate for the frustrating and growth-inhibiting supervisory relationship.

Many times, the Level 3 supervisee is beyond formal, regular supervision but will seek supervision regarding a specific case or situation. This can be especially useful if the supervisor is at or approaching Level 3 Integrated since the supervisee will then be provided a valuable model.

At this level, optimal development may be encouraged if the supervisor holds a theoretical orientation different from that of the supervisee. This is especially true if the supervisee is well-established at Level 3. Such differences promote a broadening of understanding regarding the therapeutic process. Articulating and integrating differences in terminology, constructs, and interventions serves to expand the Level 3 counselor's repertoire. The Level 3 stability and professional identity allows for this expansion without distress or disorganization.

In terms of the Loganbill, Hardy, and Delworth (1982) model, all five categories of interventions are appropriate for use with the Level 3 supervisee. Catalytic interventions—those designed to get things moving—are essential, as are the confrontative ones discussed previously. Catalytic interventions that involve varied roles for the counselor and that help the counselor to become aware of small, incremental changes in the client during therapy have proven especially useful in our work. For example, one of us worked with a new doctoral level supervisee who maintained a generally effective stance as a warm, empathic counselor. Assigned several clients with high levels of sociopathy, she became frustrated and less effective. The catalytic intervention was conceptualized by the supervisor as teaching the supervisee how to guard against manipulation in the counseling session. Discussion and role playing were used to achieve this end.

Supervisors of counselors at this level need to be aware that often their supervisees are making major professional transitions, such as into internship or the first professional position. Such transitions often cause temporary regressions in one or more structures, most especially in autonomy. In addition, such supervisees may be overwhelmed by nonclinical concerns and may request help with these issues from supervisors. Although it is essential to keep the focus of supervision on therapy work, some attention to these issues is warranted, if only for the reason that the supervisor may be the first person in the new environment with whom the supervisee establishes a relationship. Often, however, much of what is done in reference to other issues is applicable as well to counseling work.

Parallel processes, though possible at any stage, are a particularly salient issue with the Level 3 supervisee. This process is conceptualized as one in which we ascertain in supervision specific vestiges of the relationship between the supervisee and his or her client. In the case where the supervisee is also providing supervision to another trainee the parallel process between the two supervisions is often striking. Often, the Level 3 supervisee acts out with his or her supervisee an issue which is relevant in his or her own supervision. Here, Level 3 supervisees sometimes handle issues as they perceive their own supervisor would, with the lower level supervisee in effect playing out the Level 3 supervisee's role. For example, a supervisee who was experiencing some difficulty handling confrontations by her supervisor saw the same reactions in her own supervisee and backed off from a very appropriate confrontation. In explaining this to her supervisor, the Level 3 trainee expressed the belief that she had acted correctly because her supervisee was too vulnerable for the confrontation. She was unaware of her own feelings of vulnerability, which were then brought up and discussed in supervision.

The above discussion points to another important aspect of supervising the Level 3 therapist. Self-disclosure by the supervisor can be used more effectively with Level 3 trainees than with either Level 1 or 2. The Level 1 trainee often has difficulty with supervisor self-disclosure as it may appear inconsistent with the expert role (unless it is a recollection of a similar experience from the supervisor's own early training). The Level 2 trainee can benefit from properly timed self-disclosure by the supervisor but may also respond in a negative reaction toward what is perceived as condescension. The Level 3 therapist is more aware and less reactive. Therefore, supervisor self-disclosure, by making issues more salient and facilitating a collaborative approach to supervision, can be an excellent learning tool.

The Level 3 Integrated counselor is conceptualized as beyond supervision. Nevertheless, in our experience such professionals welcome opportunities to consult regarding their cases. To be most helpful, the supervisor should be functioning at the same level, but this is not universally true. For example, a Level 3 Integrated counselor working with a Hispanic client for the first time may be aided by a supervisor with special competency with this population at a lower developmental level. It is our experience that those with specific competencies in one or more domains can provide useful, specific supervisory help to counselors whose overall functioning is at a higher level. Such help has, of course, some limitations. For example, a Level 1 or Level 2 supervisor who is knowledgeable about the Hispanic culture may not be able to translate this information into suggestions useful to the Level 3 Integrated therapist. Conflict will occur if the supervisor demands specific behaviors from the supervisee without allowing implementation to be based on the supervisee's personal therapeutic style.

We have seen many changes in our trainee over the course of training. Similarly, the nature of supervisory influence has also changed. The Level 3 trainee is not as naive or uninformed as the Level 1 trainee so his or her ability to process information via the central route (carefully considered) has increased. In addition, the tenuous therapeutic self-confidence of the Level 2 trainee has developed into a more consistent and accurate self-appraisal; thus we expect less likelihood of resistance or reactance from the trainee. It is important that the supervisor be skilled and stay within her or his range of competence in supervision. Level 3 trainees are quite adept at assessing the supervisor's strengths and weaknesses and will be inclined to ignore suggestions not based on a deep understanding on the part of the supervisor.

As noted in the previous section, if this level trainee is matched with a supervisor who is at a lower level of counselor development, we can expect a boomerang effect to occur. The trainee will resist the supervisor's influence, and the perceived credibility of the supervisor will be diminished. This trainee is likely, in such situations, to seek information from other sources.

We believe that a major function of supervision for this level trainee is to point out areas of lower level functioning, as well as to encourage integration across domains. Thus, the role of the supervisor is to carefully assess the level of functioning of the trainee, confront discrepancies, and encourage exploration and integration. For this to occur, the supervisor must be sufficiently knowledgeable to guide the trainee towards this integration.

At this stage, the supervisor exerts the most influence on the supervisee through what we call the "message." If the supervisor is held in high esteem, this increases the likelihood that the trainee will listen to what the supervisor has to say. But only the accuracy and usefulness of the message can result in any attitude or behavior change by the trainee. The usefulness of the message is determined in part by the supervisor's awareness of issues currently important to the trainee, the trainee's level of development across domains, and the trainee's therapeutic and personal styles.

The role of affect is still important at this level, although the wide swings noted in the Level 2 trainee will have subsided. It remains important to assist the trainee to explore affective reactions to clients, professional roles, and career decisions. It should be remembered that certain information and impressions are more accessible to the trainee when in certain moods rather than in others. Being aware of changes in affect in the trainee, both in the supervision session and in sessions with clients, and processing reactions and alternatives while the mood is still salient assist the trainee to more completely process important information when making decisions.

A final consideration should be noted. This trainee has a vastly increased knowledge of psychotherapy and increased self-knowledge of his or her individual therapeutic style. Therefore, the need to actively guide and persuade this trainee is less than with lower level trainees. The supervision process is much more similar to a client-centered approach to counseling. The focus is more on helping the trainee derive his or her own idiosyncratic professional identity, rather than on skills or bodies of knowledge. Thus, the need to persuade is reduced, and supervision becomes more collegial. Although training remains a focus for areas where our supervisee has yet to adequately develop, supervision generally tends toward providing an environment that is both supportive of and confrontive toward the supervisee's personal and professional development. In essence, there is less that we can teach.

The supervisor of the Level 3 trainee is, then, "a supervisor for all seasons," able to offer his or her high level of functioning in service of the trainee's development. This supervisor functions at a minimum of Level 3, has a mature perspective on the field, and, above all, develops a wise sense of how and when to intervene. Supervision of a Level 3 professional is highly rewarding for those who can let go. As supervision of Level 1 trainees is similar to the training and rearing of children, and

Level 2 to the guidance of adolescents, so supervision of Level 3 counselors is comparable to the parenting of young adults. One allows and encourages the young to go off on their own but reminds them that the safe hearth of home and a listening ear are theirs for the asking.

7

Assessing
Developmental Levels of
Counselors and Therapists

The purpose of this chapter is to identify aspects of assessment in the supervision process that are particularly important for the developmental model. Various instruments and mechanisms for assessment have been described in the supervision literature, but none have been specifically designed for broad-based developmental assessments. We discuss some of the problems for researchers in devising assessment procedures and suggest several ways in which these issues can be addressed. We also note where existing instruments can be useful in the developmental model and describe additional mechanisms for helping the supervisor assess progress in trainees.

The Need for Assessment

The developmental model outlined in this book proposes guidelines for practitioners and researchers in evaluating trainees. By identifying eight domains of development and positing three structures that can be used to chart development within these domains, we have already emphasized the need to examine a number of areas in the assessment process. Indeed, in this model assessment assumes a critical role because we must alter our approach to supervision to fit the needs of the trainee. Without the ability to assess the developmental level of the trainee, we are hard pressed to provide the appropriate environment to encourage growth.

Typically, supervisors rely on the amount of experience a trainee brings into the supervisory relationship to initially assess the trainee's strengths and training needs. To some degree, the nature of past relevant experience is also evaluated in terms of the particular focus of the current clinical experience. The difficulty with this approach is our inability to evaluate the quality of the previous experiences and to gauge what benefit the trainee actually derived from them. As McNeill, Stoltenberg, and Pierce (1985) have noted, global measures of experience are at best crude indexes of development. We can better utilize listings of past experiences by specifically organizing the data into a format that reflects the areas and extent of training or practice.

Often the supervisor will rely on early impressions of the skill level of a given trainee in deciding upon the type of training experiences most appropriate at the present time. Clinical judgment can be a very effective and accurate mechanism for assessing a trainee's level of development, but without sufficient guidelines, these impressions may remain vague and global. In addition, a system is needed to guide assessment across domains so that a broader spectrum of information is considered in evaluation and planning. Thus, the clinical impressions of the supervisor need to be organized in such a way as to provide systematic and useful information for the supervision process.

We noted earlier that assessment plays an important role in developmental models of supervision because of the need for the supervisor to provide the appropriate environments for the trainee. If we expose the trainee to an environment too advanced for him or her, we will confuse the trainee and elicit excessive anxiety. On the other hand, too structured an environment will frustrate growth in the trainee, elicit boredom, or, perhaps, result in reactance. The complex view that a trainee can be at various levels for various domains demands accurate assessment across domains. It is an error for the supervisor to assume constancy across domains, and the risk of providing inappropriate environments is increased if one makes such an assumption. It is quite likely that a given supervisor will work with a trainee across a number of domains and, therefore, must be sensitive to the need to behave differently depending upon the particular focus of supervision at a given point in time.

Current Assessment Procedures

Current assessment instruments and mechanisms fall into five general categories: measures completed by the supervisor, behavioral observations, measures completed by the supervisee, client ratings, and work samples. None of these approaches to assessment is sufficient by itself, but all can be used effectively to provide important information. We first examine some of the problems and inaccuracies resulting from the use of these techniques and then suggest how they can be effectively used in a broad-based assessment.

Supervisor Measures. Quite often supervisors rely on evaluations of trainees provided by previous supervisors when planning training for a new supervisee. These evaluations may be communicated orally or in written form, but often the appraisal is not done systematically and usually is limited to both positive and negative highlights. Such evaluations give us little with which to work. Unfortunately, we are often forced to begin supervising a trainee knowing only positive or negative impressions from the previous supervisor. Although it is a common assumption that one can sort a room full of therapists into good ones and others, the danger exists that the interpretations or inferences made by a supervisor may be misleading. Consequently, we must either assume that the impressions are accurate or dismiss them and draw our own conclusions. Neither option is particularly attractive.

Another problem with relying solely on supervisor impressions is the danger of evaluations based on one theoretical orientation applied to a different orientation without an appropriate translation of techniques and intent. A supervisor who works primarily from a strict behavioral orientation, for example, may not be able to fairly evaluate the performance of a trainee working from a psychodynamic approach. Thus, we may have a trainee evaluated rather low by one supervisor but scoring high with a different supervisor.

Quite often, impressionistic supervisor evaluations are limited to specific aspects of diagnosis or therapy. A given supervisor may focus on the importance of certain interactions or processes while ignoring others. The supervisor's biases may become so pronounced that we receive evaluations—whether overly positive or overly negative—based primarily on a limited scope of interactions. This is not particularly problematic if the parameters of these evaluations are delineated. All too often, however, these focused evaluations are presented as overall assessments and can be quite misleading to the next supervisor (as well as unfair to the trainee).

Although inferences and interpretations made by the supervisor have their bases in behavior, often these behavioral benchmarks are omitted from the evaluation. Again, our reliance on clinical judgment may lead us astray if we do not know the actual behaviors used by the supervisor to form opinions about trainee characteristics or insight. For example, one of us recalls an incident where a trainee was judged by his supervisor as unable to effectively utilize feedback in the supervision session. The entire evaluation at the end of the term for this trainee, written in a narrative fashion, suggested that he had performed poorly during his practicum. The lack of agreement of this latest evaluation with earlier reports on the trainee prompted the next supervisor to investigate further. Upon inquiring into the specific behaviors that led the previous supervisor to rate the trainee poorly, it was discovered that the trainee had respectfully disagreed with an interpretation of his behavior as a personality deficiency based on a single interaction with a client. The trainee's disagreement was perceived as resistance, and a power struggle ensued. Thus, little progress was made on other issues, and a negative evaluation resulted.

In some supervision research the supervisor is asked to do self-evaluations of his or her behavior in supervision sessions. A typical format is to provide the supervisor with a general description of a prototypical trainee and then have the supervisor respond to questionnaire or open-ended items regarding the particular approach and techniques that he or she would use in working with the trainee. While this research is helpful in assessing supervisor attitudes regarding the training process, it assumes that the supervisor's actual behavior will match his or her responses. This assumption is, at best, tenuous.

Supervisor impressions can be a useful mechanism for assessing a supervisee's development. A wealth of important information can result from a systematic treatment of clinical impressions by the supervisor. These are even more helpful, and more easily validated, if behavioral examples are also included. Without these guidelines, the utility of such evaluations drops dramatically.

Behavioral Observations. The basis for the ratings discussed above is often an unsystematic observation of trainee and supervisor behavior either in counseling or supervision sessions. One way to avoid the problems mentioned above is to use behavioral coding systems that rely solely on observable and classifiable behaviors. While this addresses the problem of providing behavioral benchmarks for evaluation and assessment, other problems are introduced.

Behavioral coding systems are generally designed to be quite specific and usually rely on grouping a number of discrete behaviors into general categories. The systems suffer from trying to compromise between exhaustively covering all possible therapist and client responses and being simple enough to allow for reliable coding. Some of the systems were borrowed from related areas and have been altered to reflect the counseling or supervision process. For example, Amidon (1965) developed a system of ten counselor categories that was derived from his work in education. The system does not provide much guidance for client responses, and the counselor comments are classified as either direct or indirect. Another problem with Amidon's system, shared by others designed specifically for counseling interactions (for example, the Hill Interaction Matrix; Hill, 1965), is reliance solely on frequencies of behaviors without regard to how these behaviors were sequenced. Finally, only verbal responses are coded. No attention is paid to how these might be mediated by nonverbal behaviors.

Other systems have been developed that focus primarily on categories deemed appropriate for a superordinate model of therapy (for example, Carkhuff, 1969; Ivey, 1971). It is arguable how valid these systems are for use with other orientations. In addition, only certain theoretically important behaviors are coded; others deemed irrelevant for the model are ignored.

Holloway (1982; Holloway and Wampold, 1983) has used a variation devised by Blumberg (1970) on the Flanders (1970) system for educators. She adapted the system for supervision sessions, which resulted in sixteen categories of behaviors later reduced to eleven. The system shows promise for research purposes as it classifies both supervisor and supervisee behaviors with some reference to the sequencing of these behaviors. Like all such systems, however, different content and interaction processes are classified into the same categories, which results in a loss of usable information. In addition, nonverbal behavior is not considered seriously, so qualifiers to verbal responses tend not to be coded. With the coded behaviors, the methods of analyzing sequential interactions are incapable of identifying patterns of behaviors occurring over extended periods of time. This is a problem because, as Hill, Carter, and O'Farrell (1983) note, a particular intervention may not result in insight or observable change until some time far removed from the initial interaction or outside of the counseling or supervision session.

An additional problem with Holloway's approach, as with all of these systems, is the difficulty and time-consuming nature of the technique. Raters must be intensively trained, and a staggering amount of information must be coded and analyzed. This, of course, limits the utility of such systems for applied settings.

Advances in technology, however, may improve the usefulness of behavioral coding systems by reducing the amount of time and effort needed by coders. Currently, interaction analysis equipment is available that can interface with computers and dramatically increase the speed and accuracy of ratings. In addition, this new generation of instrumentation allows for simultaneous recording of a number of behaviors, thus improving the range and number of codable responses. Continuous measurements of time (in fractions of seconds) also allow for more exact measures of the duration of various responses. Clearly, effective use of this technology can provide considerable information for the researcher. Both verbal and nonverbal behaviors can be coded, and elaborate sequential analyses can be conducted. The usefulness of this approach for practitioners, however, remains limited in the foreseeable future.

A basic assumption of these techniques, even of the elaborate ones, is that the observed behavior is characteristic of the individuals who are interacting. This may or may not be true. For example, if one uses observations of a trainee working with one client over the course of therapy (as opposed to a single session, which is more typical), the supervisor or researcher can watch the development of the relationship and treatment plan over time. This allows for a detailed evaluation of effectiveness in this case. The interactions, however, may not be indicative of the trainee's work with other clients; the generalizability of assessment is questionable. If one chooses an alternative approach of scanning selected sessions across clients, some conclusions regarding work with various types of problems can be drawn. However, these observations are of isolated interactions and do not provide any information regarding the trainee's follow-through with treatment plans.

An additional limitation of behavioral observations from a developmental point of view is that overt behavior is not necessarily indicative of the underlying level of conceptual development. One can demonstrate certain behaviors without understanding their complexities, interactions with client dynamics, or timing considerations. These limitations are reduced, somewhat, by using complex measures of interactions within a sequential framework. Nonetheless, one should avoid relying solely on this source of information.

Supervisee Measures. This approach to supervisee assessment is the one used most often in the research literature and plays an important role in assessment in applied settings as well.

As with the approaches discussed previously, this one also has its problems.

Measures can focus on trainee self-assessment or trainee assessment of the supervisor. Regarding the former, a basic assumption is that the supervisee is adequately aware of his or her behaviors, needs, or other reactions to training experiences. We suggest that trainees, particularly lower level trainees, are likely not to be sufficiently aware or resistance-free to be able to respond consistently in an accurate manner. Depending upon the developmental level of the trainee, we expect a response set that reflects either what the trainee believes he or she is supposed to think, feel, or need or a reaction against such a demand. Often such measures include items tapping the trainee's level of satisfaction with supervision. As noted in earlier chapters, the trainee's response may be a function of how comfortable—and not how effective—supervision was. It may take some time after a particular supervision relationship has ended before the trainee can fully understand its impact on him or her.

For such assessments to be helpful, it is probably best to attempt to tap perceptions of the supervisee and to not assume that these responses necessarily reflect reality. A few instruments can be found in the literature that attempt to measure supervisee characteristics that are important to the supervision process (for example, Heppner and Roehlke, 1984; Reising and Daniels, 1983; Worthington, 1984), while others attempt to tap supervisee perceptions of the supervisor's behavior (for example, Friedlander and Ward, 1984; Zucker and Worthington, 1986). In our own work (McNeill, Stoltenberg, and Pierce, 1985; Stoltenberg, Pierce, and McNeill, 1987), we have attempted to balance the items used to examine various factors in terms of social presentation, or demand issues. It is necessary to construct self-report instruments in such a way as to not suggest to the respondent which are the desired or higher level answers. Considerable work is needed to improve the existing instruments and to develop new, more broadly based self-report assessment instruments that get at issues important to the developmental model.

Models of trainee assessment of the supervisor suffer

from most of the same limitations noted earlier regarding supervisor assessments. These assessments are usually based, to varying degrees, upon the trainee's interpretations of the supervisor's behaviors and are strongly influenced by the trainee's values in supervision. As noted previously, examining the actual behaviors may be more useful than impressions or interpretations of those behaviors, and what is valued by the trainee may not reflect what is most growth-promoting.

Client Assessment of the Trainee. Various instruments have been developed to elicit client perceptions of their counselors based either on models of important counselor characteristics (for example, the Counselor Rating Form; Barak and LaCrosse, 1975) or relationship parameters (for example, the Barrett-Lennard Relationship Inventory; Barrett-Lennard, 1964). These measures may or may not touch on the particular therapeutic orientation used by the trainee. Although they are helpful in tapping client perceptions of the therapist, it is another question as to how or whether these perceptions reflect effective or ineffective therapy. In fact, the measures are quite susceptible to change over the course of therapy. Thus, conclusions based on these measures need to be supported by other sources of information.

Client outcome measures should be used in assessing trainee competence. However, selection of such measures should be made carefully. Measures relying primarily on client reports of satisfaction with therapy are subject to the same limitations as supervisee reports of satisfaction with training. The client may react negatively to reasonable demands for movement from the therapist or may positively rate a therapist who merely provides a comfortable atmosphere. Client outcome measures need to be designed to fit the particular presenting problems, emerging problems, and life situations of the clients.

Work Samples. Actual examples of the trainee's performance in various domains can be an important element of assessment. Psychological reports, videotaped sessions with clients, case notes, written or verbal conceptualizations, and so on, provide valuable indications of a trainee's development. These work samples, however, are not without their inadequacies.

An obvious problem with work samples is that they are often tied to one particular client or session and may not accurately reflect the trainee's skill level. In addition, we occasionally encounter trainees who are quite skilled in writing but who are not so skilled in therapy. Thus, we may have convincing case write-ups or diagnostic reports that are based upon poor interviewing skills or test administration. Conversely, we may have trainees who can conduct therapy and assessment sessions well but who write them up poorly. In short, we need to know whether the work sample reflects the trainee's ability to write or his or her ability to counsel.

An additional limitation of work samples is their selective nature. A trainee may work well (or poorly) with a client in one session and work quite differently with the same client in another session. For example, one of the training programs with which we have been affiliated requires a qualifying exam in psychotherapy. This consists of a statement of therapeutic orientation by the trainee, a brief summary of the case, a detailed analysis of a therapy session, and an audiotape or videotape of the session with a transcript. We have encountered trainees who had remarkable sessions with their clients but who were unable to communicate what had occurred in writing or even to understand what they had accomplished. We have also known trainees who could convincingly articulate their orientation and present an impressive case summary, only to find that what they did in therapy had little relation to what they had written. Some trainees whom we expected, based on previous encounters in supervision, to have considerable difficulty in passing their exams performed remarkably well. Others whom we thought were superior therapists had considerable difficulty in their qualifying exams. One is left with the uncertainty of whether earlier impressions were inaccurate, growth or regression had occurred quickly in the trainee, or the trainee happened to select just the right (or wrong) client for his or her orientation and skills.

Conclusion. All of the assessment approaches discussed above have limitations that should be taken into account. In order for an accurate and useful assessment to be conducted, information collected in different ways from various sources must be utilized. Developmental theorists (for example, Hunt, 1971; Loevinger, 1976) believe that broad-based assessments are necessary in classifying individuals into developmental levels. The remainder of this chapter discusses ways to accomplish such assessments for both the researcher and the practitioner in the supervision context.

Developmental Assessment

Our model of developmental supervision requires assessment across all eight domains of professional functioning. The trainee is assessed on each of the three structures that are characteristic of therapist development; self- and other-awareness, motivation, and autonomy are used to identify the level of development of the trainee for any given domain.

The remainder of this chapter focuses on guiding principles for developmental assessment of counselor trainees. Specific forms and instruments are referred to; more detailed treatments of these are included in the Resources section at the end of the book. Resource A lists and describes various instruments useful in the assessment of supervision processes. Resource B provides a background information form for supervisees to complete prior to the start of supervision. Finally, Resource C is a case conceptualization format for use in training supervisees in the process of integrating various sources of information useful in case conceptualizations.

Some of the following material has already been presented in earlier chapters. However, we deemed it important to address assessment considerations within a single chapter as an aid to practitioners and researchers.

Fundamentals of Assessment. Evaluating the progress of trainees is not a periodic activity for the supervisor but is rather an ongoing process necessary to provide appropriate feedback and training experiences for the supervisee. While some of the assessment mechanisms discussed in the Resources are best used in a "pre-post" fashion, others are designed for continuous application. Some assessment tools are attempts at objective evaluations, while others are, out of necessity, highly subjective in nature. Some mechanisms are quantifiable, while others attempt to get at differences not readily reduced to numbers. By using both quantitative and qualitative approaches, we can increase our knowledge of the trainee and improve the supervision and training environments we provide.

As Loganbill, Hardy, and Delworth (1982) note, supervision is an inherently evaluative process. The building of a collaborative relationship between the supervisor and the trainee can, at times, appear inconsistent with evaluation and assessment. It is important, then, to establish the need for and benefits of ongoing assessments of trainee progress. We believe that assessment and evaluation need not entail negative connotations for either supervisor or trainee. It is necessary that the supervisor present the purposes of assessment at the beginning of the supervisory relationship so that the issue of evaluation is out in the open and discussed before inconsistent impressions are formed. It is in the best interests of the trainee for adequate assessment to occur on an ongoing basis. Without such assessments, proper training becomes more difficult.

We believe that the developmental model is particularly able to present evaluation in a nonthreatening manner. Rather than focusing on what is done correctly and incorrectly, as is true of some models of training, the developmental approach emphasizes growth. Although there are skills associated with various approaches to therapy that must be learned in order to effectively work with a client, the developmental model of supervision places skills and techniques in a context of progressive movement toward a desired end state. Thus, being at a particular level of development need not be seen as negative but rather viewed as the culmination of training to this point in time. It is not bad to be a Level 1 or Level 2 therapist. Rather, it is a reflection of the individual's development to date given the growth-inducing experiences provided during the course of training. One does not accuse a child of inadequacy because he or she is not yet an adult. It is the interaction of the limitations and strengths of the individual with specific training experiences that results in a particular level of development. By intentionally providing facilitative environments, we can assist the developmental process. Even with trainees who develop more slowly than others, the rate of development need not be considered a limiting factor in the degree of potential development.

Researching the Supervision Process. Holloway (1984) has discussed the importance of three aspects of supervision in researching and evaluating the effectiveness of the process: the evaluator, the focus of evaluation, and the context of evaluation. She notes four sources of evaluation: the supervisor, the trainee, the client, and objective observers. The focus of evaluation may be the supervisor, the trainee, or the client. The context of evaluation can be either the supervision or the counseling interview. There are eighteen possible combinations of these categories. Of these, ten are relevant for our purposes. These are listed in Resource A along with a compilation of instruments useful for evaluating the supervision process for each of these situations. By attending to each of these situations, a detailed picture of the trainee's functioning in intervention skills, performance of assessment techniques, and interpersonal assessment can be constructed. In addition, important information regarding other domains can be obtained.

Unfortunately, instruments capable of adequately addressing all aspects of the proposed developmental model have yet to be constructed. Brief descriptions of current instruments are provided in Resource A, however, to aid the researcher and practitioner in deciding which existing instruments may be most useful in their particular setting. We strongly recommend to supervision researchers that they use instruments addressing as many of the ten combinations of evaluator, focal person, and context of evaluation as possible when investigating the supervision process. While this approach is too time-consuming and elaborate to be used on an ongoing basis by practitioners, for investigators interested in researching the supervision process the resultant detailed data should prove very enlightening. Such extensive data, if effectively integrated, should help clarify the interactive relationship of trainee development with supervisor behavior and other environmental influences. As noted earlier, longitudinal studies, in addition to cross-sectional research, are needed to validate the developmental model.

A weakness of all of the instruments described and the format used to classify them is the lack of attention to more specific aspects of the context of performance and evaluation. The next chapter describes a model of the effects of various professional and educational settings on the development of counselors and psychotherapists.

Developmental Assessment by the Supervisor. To begin, it is necessary to collect detailed background information on the trainee. Past counseling and therapy experiences (both supervised and nonsupervised) can provide a rough indication of the opportunities the trainee has had to experience facilitative environments. The number of client contact hours the trainee has had and the extent of supervision are also important information. Of additional value is knowledge of the theoretical orientation used in any given practicum or experience, the therapeutic context (that is, type of agency, individual, group, marital, and so on), and the types of assessments used (for example, personality, vocational, intelligence). Included with this background information can be intervention skills learned and the trainee's perceptions of current strengths and weaknesses. An example of a background information form is included in Resource B. We recommend that this information be collected prior to the start of a supervision relationship. The form can be periodically updated and kept in the trainee's file, where it is accessible to each new supervisor at a given training site.

Measures of the supervisory relationship provide indications of what is needed for the current—or the subsequent—training experience and the extent of development over the course of a particular practicum or rotation. Instruments designed to measure a trainee's self-perceptions of developmental level, knowledge of theory and skills, therapeutic behaviors, assessment skills, and ability to conceptualize clients can be given at the beginning and the end of a training period. While these measures are subject to demand characteristics and falsification, they are helpful in understanding how the trainee views himself or herself at different junctures of training. One of many instruments useful in this regard is the Supervisee Needs Questionnaire (SNQ), which taps trainees' expectations regarding supervision and perceptions of current training needs. After the first two or three weeks into the term, trainees should complete a self-report instrument that describes how they see themselves both as therapists and as supervisees. The supervisor can use this to make an initial estimation of their developmental level. The Supervisee Levels Questionnaire (SLQ) is one such instrument. The supervisor might consider having the SLQ completed again at the end of the term in order to assess any changes.

Instruments addressing the supervisor's impressions of the trainee's skills and level of development can also be useful in evaluating both the current level and training needs. Such measurements are probably best taken at the end of a training experience and should be forwarded to the next supervisor for use in designing subsequent training plans. We recommend the Oetting Michaels Anchored Ratings for Therapists (OMART) instrument for this purpose. Its use of behavioral descriptions to augment anchored ratings across a number of important areas makes it the most useful single instrument for this purpose.

Finally, it is useful to collect information from the trainee at the end of the term regarding his or her perception of the effectiveness of both the supervisor and the supervision experience. In academic settings, teacher evaluations are generally required. Unfortunately, most forms used in this context are virtually useless in providing the supervisor with feedback concerning the effectiveness of supervision. The Supervisor Perception Form (form T), particularly the supervision impact subscale, should provide more useful feedback for supervisors, whether primarily in academic or applied settings. Resource A provides discussions of these and other currently available instruments we consider relevant to the developmental approach to supervision.

Work samples are necessary for professional activity and helpful in assessing trainee level. Psychological report writing is a typical activity in many training experiences, as are case notes, summaries, and therapy outcome data. These should be carefully monitored by the supervisor to ensure that good records of client treatment are maintained by the agency and that quality information is conveyed to other professionals and agencies. Client change over time is an important measure of counselor effectiveness. A rather brief instrument that is helpful for assessing change is the Current Adjustment Rating Scale (CARS). This fourteen-item scale can be used by the trainee in a "pre-post" fashion to collect clients' perceptions of therapy effectiveness.

Work samples can also serve as qualitative measures of the trainee's development in various domains. This is discussed in more detail later in this chapter. Resource C contains the Case Conceptualization Format (Loganbill and Stoltenberg, 1983), which has been useful in our supervision experience. This is a formal approach to training supervisees in conceptualizing clients and can be used as a qualitative measure of trainee development.

The constraints inherent in various instruments of assessment suggest their relative utility for applied settings versus research activities. Mechanisms used for evaluating trainee behavior in supervision and counseling sessions make this point very well. As noted earlier, behavioral coding systems can provide important information to the supervisor. Unfortunately, the amount of time needed to code behaviors effectively and analyze the resulting data renders these systems virtually useless in typical supervision settings. Their usefulness for research, however, probably justifies such an investment of time and energy. Lichtenberg and Heck (1986) and Wampold (1986) discuss some of these systems and how they can be used in research on the supervision and counseling process.

We discuss later in this chapter how the supervisor can

use observations of the trainee in a more qualitative manner to assist in assessing trainee developmental level and deciding on the effectiveness of various supervision environments. Each supervisor, however, has to decide how much time and energy should be invested in completing instruments. For less experienced supervisors, the instruments we have recommended can help in developing a clinical sense for the training process. For more experienced supervisors, periodically collecting "objective" data via these measures can serve to either validate clinical impressions or point out areas where these impressions may need to be examined.

The information collected from these various sources of assessment can be integrated into a profile of a given trainee. Figure 1 is an example of a form that may be used to categorize the trainee in developmental terms for the eight domains. For example, if the supervisor believes the trainee is at Level 1 for the structure of motivation in the domain of client conceptualization, then "Level 1" is entered in the appropriate space. Such a profile can be helpful for both the trainee and subsequent supervisors.

Of course, not all of these areas are important for all supervisory relationships. In addition, as noted earlier, instruments do not currently exist that measure each of the three structures for the three levels of development across the eight domains. Even if a complete battery of measures could address all of these areas, it would likely not be practical to use due to the considerable time required (although this might not be a drawback for researchers). To obtain additional useful information about trainee development, qualitative assessments are necessary.

Qualitative Assessment Within Domains

We now assess the three structures in three specific domains of professional activity. Although some of this information appears earlier in the book, the following discussion provides more specific guidelines for the supervisor based primarily on expected trainee behavior at each level. All eight domains

Figure 1. Counselor Development Profile.

M A DA M A DA M A DA M A DA M A DA M A DA M A DA M A DA M A DA

Note: M = Motivation, A = Awareness, DA = Dependency/Autonomy.

are important areas of professional development. However, we detail development in the following discussion for three areas of primary importance for the clinical supervisor. Intervention skills competence is discussed for each level of development. Client conceptualization and treatment goals and plans are discussed together because of their interrelatedness. This discussion is intended as an orientation to qualitative assessment that can guide the supervisor in assessing the five other domains.

Intervention Skills Competence. The developmental model described in this book primarily uses an organismic approach. The importance of growth and increasing complexity is an underlying theme. For Level 1 trainees in this domain, however, a mechanistic model is more appropriate. It is necessary for the trainee to learn basic counseling skills in order to facilitate exploration and movement on the part of the client. Thus, a skills-based approach such as Ivey's (1971) or Egan's (1986) is an effective tool in teaching these skills. Similarly, evaluation of the Level 1 counselor can be based on observational data, which should reflect the extent to which such skills have been learned. Of importance for Level 2 trainees are timing issues and experimentation with new or unusual applications of learned skills. The Level 3 counselor is characterized by integration of intervention skills effective within the individual's personal style and therapeutic orientation.

Given this brief introduction, how do we characterize trainees in this domain in terms of self- and other-awareness? The Level 1 trainee, as noted previously, exhibits a primary emotional focus on him- or herself. This is due to anxiety either from objective self-awareness or from comparing one's behavior to the idealized norms from skills training and observation of more experienced therapists. Evaluation apprehension is also likely to be present, as the trainee is concerned with both the supervisor's and the client's evaluation of his or her therapeutic skills. Such a self-focus with negative overtones makes it difficult to empathize with, or even track, the client. Cognitively, the trainee expends considerable effort in trying to remember how to perform various interventions and when they should be

used. This often interferes with the trainee's ability to understand the client's perspective. The trainee's own evaluation of
his or her effectiveness is largely a function of how well he or
she felt the interventions were performed, with little awareness
of the client's reactions to a given intervention.

The movement to Level 2 is characterized by a shift in
emotional focus from the self to the client. Experience in counseling and practice with various interventions has increased the
trainee's confidence in his or her ability to perform various
counseling behaviors. This reduces the self-focus due to early
anxiety and allows the trainee to attend to the affect of the client. Trainee comments become less instrumental and more accurate, tapping deeper emotions. In extreme cases, the trainee
may become so in touch with the client's emotional state that
he or she becomes lost in the client's misery or other affective
state. Cognitively, the Level 2 trainee is more able to understand and take the perspective of the client. Once again, the
trainee's increasing confidence in intervention techniques allows
him or her to focus more on the client without becoming confused. Summary statements are more likely to be accurate and
validated by the client, although interpretations and integrating statements are still somewhat naive and simplistic. New
skills are more easily learned and utilized. We can expect the
trainee to use a number of interventions from various orientations (depending on exposure). The application of these interventions, however, does not reflect an integrative framework
across sessions and clients. Criteria for evaluating the effective
implementation of interventions by this trainee are increasingly
based on perceptions of the client's receptivity and satisfaction.

Movement to Level 3 is characterized by integration of
intervention skills across sessions and clients. Although interventions used may be selected from different theoretical orientations, they are not applied in a random or haphazard fashion.
Rather, they reflect the underlying personalized theoretical orientation of the therapist. In terms of awareness, this counselor
is able to move into an empathic relationship with the client
and accurately reflect his or her emotional experience. In addition, the trainee can pull back and evaluate his or her own emo-

tional responses to the client. Utilizing both affective cues, the therapist is capable of experiencing from the client's perspective and understanding how others respond emotionally to the client. From a cognitive perspective, the therapist can more readily enter the phenomenological world of the client and can objectively evaluate that world. Thus, not only are summary statements by the therapist accurate most of the time but interpretations and integrations of the client's experiences more readily ring true. The Level 3 therapist evaluates the effectiveness of his or her interventions based on a personalized theoretical foundation. Thus, the appropriateness of intervention selection and timing are judged by criteria including, but not limited to, the client's immediate favorable reactions. The Level 3 therapist understands that the role of the counselor is to effectively stimulate exploration and growth, which does not always make the client feel better.

Motivation also differs across levels. For the Level 1 trainee we expect high motivation to learn how to do therapy correctly. There is strong desire to increase one's armamentarium of counseling skills. The trainee will be champing at the bit to see real clients, as opposed to role playing with peers. As exposure to competing orientations increases, the trainee is often motivated to learn as many techniques as possible to be sure that he or she will have the one right for a given client and situation.

Life as a therapist becomes more complicated as training experiences expand and the trainee is exposed to clients exhibiting more resistance or more severe pathology. Thus, the Level 2 trainee becomes aware of the limitations of therapy and finds that simply pulling techniques out of the hat does not always produce movement in the client. The inevitable confusion and uncertainty that accompanies feeling ineffective with a client can have negative effects on the trainee's motivation for conducting therapy and for sharing his or her uncertainties or "failures" with the supervisor. The supervisor might also note some resistance on the part of the trainee to learning or using new or different techniques. This often occurs when the trainee is experiencing some success with his or her clients. The resistance

to other interventions is based upon fear of new failures or decreased self-esteem as a therapist if the trainee is unable to effectively perform the requested intervention. In addition, the
trainee may try to protect the fragile sense of professional integration he or she may occasionally experience during this stage
from the critical scrutiny of the supervisor for fear that it will
disintegrate into more confusion and uncertainty.

The Level 3 therapist is characterized by a more consistent level of motivation across clients and sessions. He or she
realizes that there are peaks and valleys during the course of
therapy and that progress is sometimes a slow process. A collection of interventions that fit well with the overriding theoretical orientation, as well as with the therapist's own personality characteristics, is used consistently. The Level 3 therapist
does not feel overly threatened by periods of lack of clarity regarding a given client. Rather, such experiences stimulate a
more complete use of the skills that have been acquired over
the course of training and practice.

As is true of self- and other-awareness and motivation,
the structure of autonomy is different at different levels. Due
to a lack of experience and understanding of effective interventions, the Level 1 trainee is quite dependent on the supervisor. The trainee must rely on the supervisor for direction and
training in the skills necessary to function adequately with clients. Thus, the selection of intervention skills to be learned is
largely left to the discretion of the supervisor. Similarly, evaluation of how well these skills have been learned and implemented is relegated to the supervisor. Supervisors can expect
numerous requests for advice on which skills should be used at
which times and for feedback on how effectively those skills
were implemented. In the extreme case, the trainee will want
a detailed scenario of which skills should be used in what order
with a given client.

The Level 2 trainee can effectively perform a number of
interventions. At times, particularly when the trainee feels in-
effectual, he or she will act much like the Level 1 trainee and
want detailed advice on what to do and how to do it. At other
times, the trainee will desire more independence of action in

counseling and supervision. These are early attempts at testing one's ability to conduct therapy independent of the supervisor. We may note some negative independence during this stage if the trainee feels his or her attempts at developing autonomy are being met with resistance by the supervisor. The tenuous professional self-esteem of this trainee can produce large shifts in the desire for autonomous functioning. In a sense, the Level 2 trainee is a bit of Level 1 and some of Level 3, minus the integration of skills. The dependency of Level 2 is less extreme and more temporary. The independence, however, is less grounded in a firm sense of professional identity and is more a function of the desire for such integration and identity than of its actuality.

Level 3 independent functioning is based upon a firm sense of professional identity. Individuals at this stage understand their personal and professional strengths and limitations and the effectiveness of therapy. The Level 3 therapist seeks consultation when needed, makes appropriate referrals, but retains responsibility for decision making.

Concepts and Plans. Table 1 integrates the domains of client conceptualization and treatment goals and plans. In a very true sense, none of the eight domains are entirely discrete. All interact with other domains to varying degrees. Nonetheless, these two areas blend together to produce a road map for the therapist.

A Final Point. During Level 1, all three domains (intervention skills, client conceptualization, and treatment goals and plans) are conceptualized as fairly discrete processes resulting in discrete products. For the Level 1 trainee, tools are often perceived as most important. Thus, skills in working with clients are of primary interest. During Level 2, understanding and empathizing with the client's experiencing enters the forefront. Skills are viewed as mechanisms through which the trainee elicits important perceptions from the client. Certain techniques may be viewed unfavorably as manipulative or sterile. For the Level 3 therapist, various skills are necessary to elicit informa-

Table 1. Client Conceptualizations and Treatment Plans.

Level 1

Self- and Other-Awareness—Emotional and cognitive self-focus. *Indications:* Diagnoses/conceptualizations will be "canned" or stereotypical, trying to fit clients into categories. Incomplete treatment plans will focus on specific skills or interventions, often quite similar across clients. Treatment plans may not reflect diagnoses.

Motivation—High, with strong desire to learn to become effective diagnostician and therapist. *Indications:* Willing student, will seek out additional information from books, colleagues, and other sources.

Autonomy—Dependent. *Indications:* Relies on supervisor for diagnoses and treatment plans. Locus of evaluation rests with supervisor.

Level 2

Self- and Other-Awareness—Emotional and cognitive focus on the client. *Indications:* Realizes treatment plan is necessary and logical extension of diagnosis. May resist "labeling" client into diagnostic classifications. Treatment plans may prove difficult due to lack of objectivity. May reflect various orientations yet lacks integration.

Motivation—Fluctuates depending upon clarity regarding various clients. *Indications:* May be pessimistic, overly optimistic or confident at times.

Autonomy—Dependency-autonomy conflict. *Indications:* May depend upon supervisor for diagnoses and treatment plans for difficult clients, may avoid or resist supervisor suggestions concerning others. Confident with some less confusing clients. More resistance to perceived unreasonable demands of supervisor, threats to tenuous independence and therapeutic self-esteem.

Level 3

Self- and Other-Awareness—Emotional and cognitive awareness of client and self. *Indications:* Able to "pull back" affectively and cognitively, monitor own reactions to client. The client's perspective and a more objective evaluation will be reflected in conceptualizations. Treatment plans will flow from diagnoses, taking into account client and environmental characteristics. Reflects therapist's own therapeutic orientation.

Motivation—Consistently high, based upon greater understanding of personality-learning theory and self. *Indications:* Not as susceptible to pessimism or undue optimism. Diagnoses and treatment plans consistently thought through and integrated.

Autonomy—Independent functioning. *Indications:* Seeks consultation when necessary. Open to alternative conceptualizations and treatment approaches but retains responsibility for decisions. Makes appropriate referrals.

---

tion from the client important for deriving complete and accurate conceptualizations and treatment plans. Other skills—or
the timing of various interventions—are deemed important for
carrying out the planned course of treatment.

Perhaps comparing this process of development with that
of a carpenter may be helpful. The apprentice carpenter is concerned with learning how to use various tools of the trade. Developing technical proficiency is necessary to carry out the in-
structions of the master carpenter. After a certain level of
proficiency has been reached, more attention can be paid to
learning about formulas and structural requirements necessary
for various projects. Finally, as the trainee approaches a master
carpenter, an understanding of how to integrate structural and
building concepts with various technical approaches to construction develops.

A danger in defining eight domains of therapist development is that they may be considered wholly separate activities.
Our intent is to identify important aspects of professional development. As we have previously stated, trainees can develop at
different rates within these domains. The integration of functioning within each domain with the others is part of the developmental process. The product of this process is a professional
who is able to organize various skills and concepts into a unified
whole that forms the boundaries of professional behavior in the
field of counseling and psychotherapy.

The complexity of this approach presents problems in objective assessment of the trainee. Although we have discussed a
number of mechanisms for evaluating trainee progress, no unified battery of assessment devices currently exists. Until future
research produces such a battery, it is up to the supervisor to decide which of the current instruments best suits his or her particular needs in a given educational, health, or agency setting. The
information derived from these instruments must be integrated
with qualitative clinical impressions formed by the supervisor
through interactions with the trainee, observations of performance, and examination of work samples. A resultant developmental profile of the trainee—one that includes the appropriate
number of domains given the nature of the supervision experi-

ence—should then be communicated to the trainee and subsequent supervisor. This information can then be used to construct the next learning environment for the trainee.

The next chapter gives additional information and guidelines for conceptualizing trainee development in various training settings.

8

How the Training Environment Affects Professional Development

We have thus far conceptualized the environment of the supervisee primarily as the supervisor, following the developmental focus of Dewey and others (see Chapter One). Kurt Lewin and his followers push us further. As early as 1936, Lewin argued that the first step in understanding human behavior—whether of individuals or of groups—is to examine the opportunities and constraints of their environments. His classic formulation—$B =$ f (P, E)—asserts that behavior (B) is a function of the interaction of certain characteristics of the person (P) and related characteristics of the environment (E). In the area of clinical supervision, Hogan (1964) and Ekstein and Wallerstein (1972) stress the importance of the total context within which supervision occurs. More recently, Reising and Daniels (1983, p. 243) ponder whether "what are commonly known as trainee characteristics may well be discovered to describe person-environment complexes and not trainees alone."

Setting—or the larger context of supervision—merits our attention and understanding if we are to accurately conceptualize both trainee development and the process of supervision. In this chapter, we first delineate several basic constructs relating to environments. We also discuss implications for supervision. We then introduce a model that we believe can be used in supervision to facilitate understanding of the interactions between trainees and their supervisory contexts. Lastly, we discuss more specifically the impact of settings on trainees.

Constructs and Theory

The biological ecology that began at the beginning of the twentieth century gave rise to a human ecology about twenty years later. Both biological and human ecology share a number of assumptions about the world based on the interdependence, adaptation, and vulnerability to the environment of all living organisms. In 1944, Kurt Lewin suggested a study of psychological ecology based solely on people's perceptions rather than on any actual features of the environment.

It remained for two associates of Lewin's, Roger Barker and Herbert Wright, to assert a full-scale ecological approach to the study of human behavior and experience. They proposed the preparation of maps of "psychological habitats" similar to biologists' maps of plant and animal habitats. These maps would include the everyday social and physical environments that surround people and affect their behavior, perceptions, and feelings. Their ideas are most fully developed in a 1978 book, *Habitats, Environments, and Human Behavior,* which pulls together the major results of twenty-five years of research at the Midwest (Kansas) Field Station. Barker and Wright set the stage for the field of ecological psychology and are its most prominent actors.

Ecological psychology starts with Barker and Wright's construct of "behavior setting," or the social and physical situations in which human behavior occurs. According to the ecological viewpoint, people are only one component of the larger behavior-setting system, a system which restricts the range of individual behavior by promoting (sometimes demanding) certain actions and by discouraging or prohibiting others. For instance, Barker and Wright found that the behaviors of children could be predicted more accurately from knowledge of the situations the children were in than from knowledge of individual characteristics of the children. As a readily recognizable example of this concept, graduate students (whatever their individual differences) all sit and take out writing materials when entering the behavior setting of a class.

Another important idea in ecological psychology is that behavior settings represent the most immediate and most behaviorally significant human environments. Thus, the approach to understanding a community or an organization is to identify and describe its relevant behavior settings.

A third key concept is that behavior settings depend on people to carry out the activities essential to the setting, and that when the number of people present is either too small or too large to permit the setting to function normally, adjustments must be made. Barker refers to behavior settings with fewer than optimal inhabitants as undermanned and notes that persons in these settings are both more active and more involved in a greater variety of actions. Indeed, the often touted virtue of small schools is that they allow greater participation by students in a variety of activities. Our students report more opportunities for initiative and action in undermanned service agencies in which client demands exceed the resources of the system.

A number of other approaches have developed within the broad fields of ecological psychology and social ecology to examine person-environment interaction. The most useful for our purposes are the subcultural approach, Holland's theory, and Pervin's transactional approach. Key constructs from these approaches are useful in considering the supervisory context.

Subcultural Approach. These approaches, articulated mainly by Clark and Trow (1966) and Newcomb, Joenig, Flacks, and Warwick (1967), are primarily concerned with identifying attitudinal or behavioral dimensions along which persons tend to vary. Thus, members of a particular subculture tend to behave in similar ways, consistent with their shared understanding or perception of the environment. In this sense, subcultures may be seen as large behavior settings.

These models have been applied mainly with college students, as in Clark and Trow's (1966) identification of four student subcultures (Academic, Nonconformist, Collegiate, and Vocational). One problem with this approach is its failure to differentiate between a personality type—that is, personality characteristics common to individuals, somewhat independent of their environment (see Holland's theory, below)—and a subculture, which is an environmental concept. One value of this approach is that it reminds us that the attitudes, values, and behaviors that motivate a person to enter and interact in an environment (subculture) may be reinforced by experiences in the environment. That is, subcultural value reinforcement may provide support both for individual stability and for directional movement toward goals consistent with the subculture. Implications for group supervision (see Chapter Nine) seem clear. It also appears that the student who encounters a differing subculture in a practicum agency setting may perceive less support and approval in that setting.

Holland's Theory. John Holland (1966) presents a theory in which human behavior is a function both of the individual's personality and of the environment in which he or she lives. Holland defines six basic personality types: Realistic, Investigative, Social, Conventional, Enterprising, and Artistic. He believes that an individual's dominant type is essentially the product of his or her life history. While persons generally possess characteristics of all six types, each individual behaves in a manner more strongly reflecting one or two orientations than the others. The more closely a person resembles a particular type, the more likely it is that he or she will exhibit personal characteristics and behaviors consistent with that type. Environments may be characterized in the same manner; for each personality type there is a related environment. Holland hypothesizes that Investigative types search for Investigative environments, and so on. In this theory, congruent person-environment matches result in positive outcomes, such as a good vocational choice, stability, and achievement, as well as personal stability, creative performance, and personal development.

Holland's theory is well known to all students of vocational behavior and career choice. It is less often applied to other areas, although Hogan and Busch (1984) urge us to consider it a major theory of personality. Important for us in terms of clinical supervision is the idea of optimal matches for our students, whether in agency settings or between supervisee and supervisor. For example, we have noted the frequent complaints of our Investigative students when placed in Social practicum settings where no research is conducted and staff interest in research findings is minimal.

Transactional Approach. The approach of Lawrence Pervin (1968) focuses on the transactions and interactions that occur between the individual and the environment. Interactions are defined as cause-effect relationships and transactions as reciprocal relationships. Pervin believes that for each individual there are interpersonal and non-interpersonal environments that tend to match the individual's personality characteristics. A match of individual to environment probably contributes to a higher degree of performance and satisfaction. Pervin hypothesizes that high performance and satisfaction result from environments that reduce the discrepancies between the individual's perceived self and his or her perceived ideal self. A key point is that an individual may be more satisfied and productive in an environment that does not offer an exact fit. The concept of challenge is essential here.

Thus, we face the notion of reasonable fit between our trainees and their supervisors and other training settings. Students frequently comment on the sense of satisfaction and mastery they achieve in a supervisory context that fits in some ways and stretches them in others.

Supervision in Context

These theories suggest a reasonable match between individuals' characteristics and the environments entered. What does this mean for the supervision enterprise? As a start, it means we must expand our model beyond the dyad—of supervisor and trainee—and the triad—of supervisor, trainee, and client—that have been the focus of our attention thus far; we must add the setting in which the training occurs. Our thinking must include at least four entities:

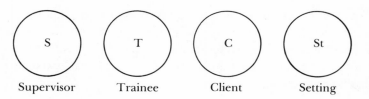

Supervisor   Trainee   Client   Setting

For student trainees, a fifth entity—the professional training program—is included.

Training Program

Each of these elements is important in supervision. The supervisor has a responsibility to facilitate the trainee's abilities as a therapist but also has responsibilities for client welfare. The trainee is focused on his or her development as a counselor but also has responsibilities to the client. The client, of course, is attempting to solve problems and function more effectively. All must function in the context of the setting, which is a mix of organizational policies, procedures, persons, and norms that allows the work to get done. The setting demands certain behaviors from the supervisor, the trainee, and the client and, in return, offers effective service and training. While the setting is usually represented by one administrator, in reality it includes all those who develop, impart, and enforce its policies and norms. Generally, this includes a number of personnel, especially support (clerical) staff. For students, the training program develops and enforces a set of expectations and norms regarding the process and outcome of the supervisory enterprise.

None of this is unfamiliar to the trainee or to the experienced supervisor. Supervisees often are aware of differences among settings that affect their experience in supervision, regardless of their supervisor. Beginning supervisors sometimes tell us stories of the ways in which the setting, often to their surprise, limits or enhances the work they do with their super-visees. "War stories" abound, but, in our experience, neither trainees nor supervisors possess tools that would allow them to make sense of the elements involved and to use them to pro-duce optimal supervisory experiences. The first tool, we believe, is the realization that the supervisory setting and (often) the training program are key components. The next step is to con-ceptualize relationships among these and ways in which the rela-tionships get played out, for better or for worse. One method of doing this follows.

Visualizing the Context: The SIC Model

After a good deal of discussion regarding issues of con-text and person-environment fit, one of us and a group of seven doctoral students developed a visual model to express our ideas and push some of our notions further. This model, originally called the BRAMJUPS (taken from the first letter of each of our names), became a vehicle to help us move beyond the super-visory dyad and look at both transactions and interactions across components. We subsequently renamed our concepts the Supervision-in-Context (SIC) Model, for ease of communication.

The SIC is a perceptual instrument drawn by the super-visee or supervisor to indicate his or her perceptions of the wider supervisory context. It is composed of both components and functions.

Components. There are three components: circles repre-senting elements in the process; contents within elements; and arrows indicating interactions or transactions among elements. We assume the five units or elements presented earlier:

1. supervisor (S)
2. trainee (T)
3. client (C)
4. setting (St)
5. training (academic) program (TP) (may or may not be rele-vant)

Contents within units or elements vary according to theoretical framework and specific purpose in using the model. Contents generally relevant to our understanding are:

all units   expectations, role, purpose
1 and 2   competencies, developmental level (including ethics)
3   competencies, developmental level (for example, cognitive, ego, moral), specific problem
4 and 5   structure, norms, facilities

Developmental level differs for units 1, 2, and 3. For unit 1 (supervisor), it refers to level as a supervisor (see Chapter Nine). For unit 2 (trainee), it refers to the level of counselor development discussed so far in this book. For unit 3 (client), it refers to level of development in cognitive, ego, or moral spheres as defined by relevant theory.

Arrows indicate interactions by unidirectionality and transactions by dual directionality (using Pervin's definition). Thus, an interaction by the agency to the trainee focusing on role would look like this:

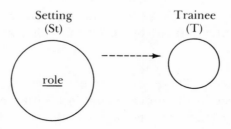

Function. Units, contents, and messages vary in saliency and relatedness. Saliency or perceived importance is indicated by the size of circles and arrows. The relationship of units is represented by relative position. Thus, an important unidirectional message regarding role from a distant and powerful setting would be drawn as:

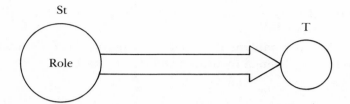

Utility. This visual model can be used in a number of ways to clarify issues of person-environment fit. One use is to have trainees draw the units, relevant contents, and arrows describing their total supervisory context. In completing such an exercise, one student was able to understand and articulate his sense of frustration for the first time. His SIC looked like this:

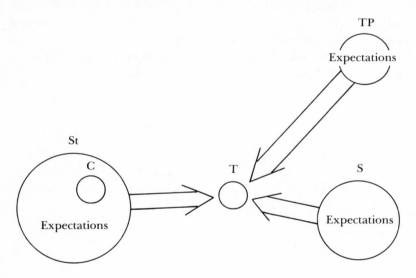

The trainee, who was a practicum student, perceived himself outside the agency in which the client was encapsulated. In addition, his supervisor had little contact with either the agency or the training program. Both the agency and the supervisor were powerful, and both were seen as sending strong messages regarding expectations. The training program, although more distant and less influential, was also perceived as sending unidirectional messages. No wonder that the student felt conflicted and frustrated!

Another student depicted her situation as one in which she felt overwhelmed by united and strong forces:

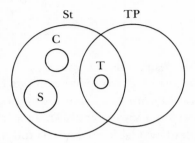

In this case, the trainee felt captive in both the setting and the training program and distant from both supervisor and client, who are perceived as the setting's property.

It can be very helpful for both supervisor and trainee to draw a SIC. For one dyad, the drawings looked like this:

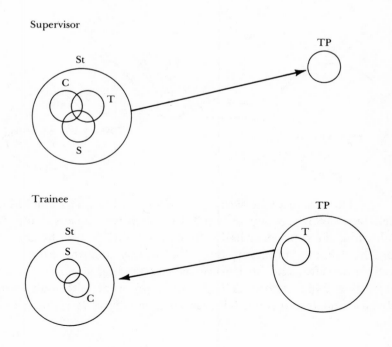

In this case, the supervisor felt connected with both trainee and client in a powerful setting, sending messages to a distant, smaller training program. The trainee, however, felt encapsulated in a powerful training program that sent messages to the less salient setting where the supervisor and the client resided. These perceptual scenarios allowed the supervisor and the trainee to first identify how they saw things and then to work toward a more mutually satisfactory arrangement. In this case, the supervisor acknowledged the power of the training program and began to work more closely with it. The trainee was able to move into a more balanced relationship with supervisor, client, and setting. Transactions replaced interactions.

The model can be used to deal with specific concerns. For example, a trainee who drew the following in terms of the purpose content only was able to identify his frustrations regarding the supervisor's and setting's roles.

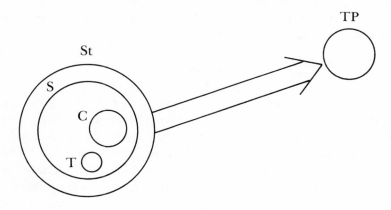

While further discussion was needed to clarify specific issues, it was clear that the trainee saw himself encapsulated by the setting and supervisory roles and as functioning as a small and insignificant part of the context.

One can also use this model to examine contents from differing theoretical constructs, such as perceived Holland types. One such rendition—that of the "I" (Investigative) student in an "S" (Social) setting—might look like this:

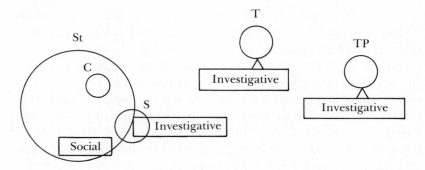

In this case, the student feels mismatched with a powerful environment and quite distant from less salient allies—the training program and the clinical supervisor.

However used, the model is valuable in enabling trainees and supervisors to conceptualize the total supervisory context in a way that can lead to more in-depth understanding and creative action. It may be useful for setting administrators as well. As a perceptual device, it inherits the subjectivity of such procedures. But it can still be useful in the clinical situation.

Settings

It is our experience that trainees, especially as graduate students, spend little time carefully considering the influence of the setting or agency in which they are seeing clients. They may complain about a specific procedure or facility, but rarely do they consider the setting in any organized way. Yet, at another level, they are very aware of settings and the interactions among the units in the total supervisory context. Thus, they tend to be acted upon by the setting (interaction) and may react with confusion, withdrawal, or anger. Some of this affect is often transferred to the supervisor if he or she is a staff member in the setting or to the training program that placed the student in that setting. Rarely is an attempt made to conceptualize the setting in some organized and relevant fashion and thus to make real the option of a transactional relationship between setting and supervisee.

A number of models that look at settings are available. Barker's behavior-setting construct has been applied by Wicker (1979) to service settings. As one part of the conceptual analysis, Wicker focuses on reactions of staff and clients to the common problem of understaffing and overpopulation. He notes that explanations for why the setting is not adequately staffed and populated help determine what actions individuals take to deal with their situations. Thus, a staff member who believes other workers are not doing their part may urge them to do more. A manager may use a variety of strategies to cope with the situation, including regulating clients' entrance into the setting or the time that clients may spend in the setting. Wicker notes that the duration of such a condition affects people's reactions. Maslach's (1978) burned-out syndrome is viewed by Wicker as the response of staff members to a prolonged situation of understaffing and overpopulation.

Trainees who enter such a setting may make a number of attributions based on staff behavior. That is, staff may be perceived as lacking empathy for clients and viewing clients in a stereotypical manner. A more careful analysis, such as Wicker proposes, would allow the trainee to view the situation as a setting issue rather than as a problem of poorly motivated staff. This type of analysis fosters more potentially productive transactions with the setting.

In addition to using a model to understand settings, there are specific characteristics of settings that affect trainees and that they should consider carefully. Among the most important are: disciplinary mix; staff roles; ease of entrance and exit for clients; and amount of structure. Most often, in selecting a setting for field experience, trainees focus on the types of clients served. This is certainly an important variable but is by no means a total indicator of fit. Some students at some phases of training find a good match in settings that are relatively open and unstructured. Others, because of individual characteristics or developmental level, are consistently frustrated and overwhelmed in such settings.

Given our developmental approach, we choose to place Level 1 trainees in settings that are relatively structured, that have a method to assign appropriate clients to the trainee, and that probably have a limited number of professional disciplines represented on the staff. Appropriate and fairly close transactions with the training program are important here. A good fit for the Level 1 trainee might look like this:

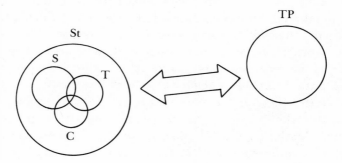

The supervisor is somewhat larger than the trainee, and both fit closely together and with the client.

As the trainee moves into Level 2, one or more of these components can be altered. Placing a trainee who is entering Level 2 in a highly ambiguous, open, unstructured, and multidisciplinary setting will almost certainly exacerbate the conflicts and confusion characteristic of Level 2. The trainee may be too overwhelmed to stick with it and may escape back to the certainty of Level 1. Or the trainee may become disenchanted with counseling altogether. Thus, the training program should still be fairly influential, although somewhat more distant. The supervisor and trainee become more equal in size and overlap less. The supervisor is less involved with the client. The scenario might look like this:

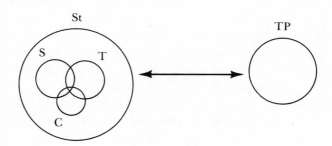

At Level 3, a good fit might involve both more distance from the training program and more separation between the supervisor and the trainee:

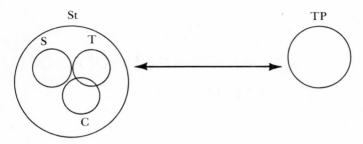

Matters of individual preference are also important. Some people enjoy the give-and-take of a setting that employs persons from diverse professions or disciplines. Others prefer to work with colleagues with similar training. What is important is that these issues are considered as selections and assignments to settings are made.

Whatever conceptual model is adhered to, consideration of context provides for a more comprehensive and accurate picture of supervision. In fields in which an intrapsychic focus is basic—such as professional psychology—looking beyond the individual trainee and the supervisory dyad is very rewarding. As supervisors, we need to be aware that we do not constitute the total environment. Barker's behavior settings, the subcultural approach, Holland's types, and transactional constructs can each prove useful in looking at the total supervisory environment. We hope that these approaches used in a clinical context will lead to research specific to the context of supervision.

As supervisors, we can often be of most help to our trainees by facilitating their understanding of the total context. With such understanding, we and they can formulate and implement transactions that are productive and rewarding. We can then, in Sarason's (1972, p. xiii) words, "venture forth with a sensitive grasp of social realities."

9

Applying the Developmental Approach to Supervisors

The development of effective supervisors is an important theme in the supervision literature, both in the past and presently. Kell and Mueller (1966, p. 99) note that "a fortunate choice of parents and a reasonably good hurdling of the developmental tasks of growing up are most helpful" in becoming an effective supervisor. They add, however, "that supervisors, as is true of counselors and clients, can learn, change, and develop qualities which they may be initially lacking." More recently, Russell, Crimmings, and Lent (1984) question the often implicit assumption that an effective therapist will also be an effective supervisor. They note that "learning to be an effective supervisor may demand knowledge and skills beyond those used in counseling" (p. 625). They believe that students should "study the supervision literature and have experiential training opportunities to develop supervisory skills." Loganbill, Hardy, and Delworth (1982) advocate training both for students and for professionals who are already supervising.

In practice, Hess and Hess (1983) report that only one-third of internship sites accredited by the American Psychological Association provide training for clinical supervisors, and only 20 percent of training directors in such settings consider this training "quite important." Bernard (1981, p. 740) cites supervisor training as a "relatively new concept" and applauds efforts of graduate programs to include education in this area. Indeed, a number of training approaches have begun to appear in the literature (for example, Bernard, 1981; Boyd, 1978; Forsyth and Ivey, 1980; Glenwick and Stevens, 1980; Kagan, 1980; Wasik and Fishbein, 1982). Russell, Crimmings, and Lent (1984) note that there appears to be some consensus on core skills for supervisors but much less agreement on higher-order competencies.

We are at a point where both specification of supervisory effectiveness and training for supervisors are recognized as important issues. Much more research in these areas is needed. Here we use our developmental perspective to address the issue of effective supervisors—their qualities, training, and development.

In this chapter, we propose levels of supervisor development largely analogous to our levels of supervisee development. We discuss issues of supervisor and supervisee match and supervisor assessment. We then propose a training model and discuss research implications of such a model. Lastly, we briefly discuss group and peer supervision.

The Supervisor: Research Findings

There is no coherent, agreed upon model of supervisor development. However, there are cues in the research literature that point us in certain directions. Pierce and Schauble (1970) found that trainees whose supervisors displayed high levels of empathy, regard, genuineness, and concreteness also rated high in these qualities. Trainees with supervisors who had low levels of these attributes showed a decrease in these qualities. A nine-month follow-up study showed the same results (Pierce and Schauble, 1971). Lambert (1974), who studied supervisor facilitative functioning in counseling versus supervision, found that supervisors offered higher levels of empathy and specificity to their clients than they did to their supervisees. No differences were found for genuineness and respect. Stone (1980) found that experienced supervisors (postintern graduate students) generated more planning statements than inexperienced supervisors (introductory psychology students) and that these statements were more focused on the trainee.

It seems reasonable at this point to believe that higher functioning supervisors are more effective and that, as with counseling skills, training may improve supervisor functioning. A description of supervisor levels helps set the stage for a discussion of appropriate training.

Training Model: Levels

In Chapter Two, we discussed the various roles of the supervisor and concluded that all had value, depending on the developmental level of the supervisee. The supervisor often starts out as teacher, consultant, and evaluator and later develops the roles of master therapist and therapist for the supervisee. Our model assumes that what distinguishes more advanced supervisors is their access to a wide variety of roles, depending on what is needed by the trainee. Less advanced supervisors have only one or two roles available to them.

In our model, progression in levels as a supervisor assumes progression in levels of counselor development. That is, we do not see the possibility of a Level 3 supervisor who is, at the same time, a Level 1 counselor. However, a Level 3 counselor supervising for the first time is likely to be at Level 1 or Level 2 in our supervisory model. The idea here is that supervision, although similar to counseling, is itself a unique process with specific knowledge, skills, and attitudes.

We hypothesize a three level (plus integrated) model for supervisors similar to that of the counselor model. Domains of the supervisor model are more problematic, however. While the eight proposed for the counselor model appear relevant, there are undoubtedly more supervision-specific domains as well. Their explication awaits further thinking and research.

Level 1. Supervisors at this level tend to be either highly anxious or somewhat naive. They, like Level 1 trainees, are anxious to do the "right" thing and be effective in the role.

They often tend toward a fairly mechanistic approach to supervisory tasks and may play a strong "expert" role with the supervisee. In terms of structures, they are highly motivated, fairly dependent on their own supervisor for help (or their recollections of how they have been supervised), and generally more aware of their own reactions than of their supervisees'. A typical Level 1 supervisor, recounting a supervisory session to a colleague, concentrates on how well he or she did as a supervisor. These supervisors take real pride in coming up with appropriate conceptualizations or interventions for supervisees to use. They talk a good deal about their supervision with their own supervisor and with colleagues and require considerable support for their work in this area. They tend to provide moderate to high structure and are quite concerned with the success of their trainees. In addition, depending on their own level of counselor development, there is often a real investment in getting the trainee to adopt their therapeutic orientation and techniques.

Assuming that these supervisors are functioning at Level 3 or at least "late" Level 2 as counselors, they can do an adequate or even good job with Level 1 supervisees. We have noticed in our own work not only that Level 1 supervisors who are themselves Level 2 counselors often provide adequate supervision to Level 1 trainees, but that the necessary task of aiding the trainee with cognitive formulations helps the supervisor to work through some of his or her own Level 2 confusion. In our experience, some Level 2 trainees are far better supervisors (provided they are matched with Level 1 supervisees) than they are counselors. The Level 2 counselor who is also a Level 1 supervisor often finds that the need to provide basic structure for the beginning supervisee helps to resolve some of his or her own confusion and ambivalence.

Level 1 supervisors have great difficulty with Level 2 trainees. In our experience, this is always a bad match. At best, it pushes the supervisor toward Level 2. It still results in a poor experience for the supervisee, however (and probably for the supervisor as well). There is just no feasible way for the Level 1 supervisor to deal with the conflict and confusion of a Level 2 trainee. What often happens is that both parties wait out the period of supervision, and little of consequence occurs. One Level 2 practicum student reported "just getting along" once she realized that her intern level supervisor was threatened by her confusion and fluctuating motivation.

A Level 3 trainee matched with a Level 1 supervisor will also just wait out the time or possibly look elsewhere for help. There is also danger of regression to Level 2, especially in motivation. One such trainee reported starting to lose her own recently acquired consistent motivation when confronted with an insecure, highly structured Level 1 supervisor. Her solution was to seek additional informal supervision from another staff member.

Level 2. The Level 2 supervisor resembles the Level 2 counselor in terms of confusion and conflict. The supervisor now sees that the process of supervision is more complex and multidimensional than he or she had imagined. It is no longer the "great adventure" it once was. Motivation fluctuates, especially in settings where the supervision function is not rewarded. The supervisor may focus heavily on the supervisee and may lose the objectivity required to provide necessary confrontation and guidance. There is a tendency to "go on one's own" in supervising, with occasional lapses into dependency on a trusted supervisor or colleague. One experienced supervisor recalls, "I was a new doctoral level staff member, supervising for only the second time. I started out with lots of enthusiasm for the job and for being a supervisor, but I lost it quickly. I felt alienated in the agency, and it was easy to identify with my supervisee and complain about everything." We have seen this reaction many times, perhaps because often the Level 2 supervisor is just beginning his or her professional career and is typically supervising in a new setting.

The Level 2 supervisor may also tend to either get angry at or withdraw from the supervisee. One of our colleagues recalls blaming the trainee for all of her own problems as a supervisor at this point. Thus, the trainee may find it difficult to arrange a session with his or her supervisor, and the lack of investment by the supervisor may be quite obvious.

Luckily for all concerned, Level 2 tends to be short-lived for most supervisors. Most are functioning at Level 3 as counselors and use this fact to push themselves on as supervisors, especially with the help of their own supervisor. Those who linger in this level often withdraw from the supervisory role. Many times supervisees are not assigned to these supervisors because they are judged not to be sufficiently motivated and effective. Also, the disruption characteristic of this level is more muted in the supervisor role than in the counselor role, perhaps because the supervisor role is viewed as less central. (One can decide, in most cases, not to serve as a supervisor and still maintain a strong identity as a counselor and therapist.) In addition, there is often less formal evaluation of the supervisor than of the trainee, making it easier to mask the Level 2 conflicts.

The Level 2 supervisor is a poor match for any supervisee but does best with a beginning Level 1 trainee. This trainee tends to elicit a protective stance that results in more consistent behavior by the supervisor. Matches with a beginning Level 2 trainee sometimes work if the supervisor is both actively aware of and working through Level 2 issues.

Level 2 supervisors need consistent and expert supervision to facilitate their own development and to provide for the welfare of their supervisees. Techniques such as cosupervision (by the Level 2 supervisor and his or her supervisor) may be productively used.

Level 3. In our opinion, most supervisors reach this level. Some stagnate at Level 1, some drop out at Level 2, but the majority go on to achieve the stable functioning characteristic of Level 3. At this level, the supervisor displays a consistent motivation toward the supervisory role and is interested in improving his or her performance, while viewing supervision as one role among many she or he has as a professional. The supervisor is functionally autonomous at this point but may seek consultation or regular supervision if circumstances warrant. This supervisor is aware of the trainee—as well as of himself or herself—and able to balance personal needs with both those of the trainee and of the setting. Differing supervisory roles though perhaps not completely integrated, are felt as more comfortable. Generally, the supervisor at this level can make an honest self-appraisal of strengths and weaknesses and will state preferences for type of supervisees. For example, one of our colleagues, aware of his ongoing difficulties with conflict, prefers to supervise either Level 1 or Level 3 supervisees.

The Level 3 supervisor probably represents the majority of those practicing supervision. He or she is able to supervise trainees at any level. However, this supervisor may be most comfortable and do his or her best work with supervisees at a specific level. The Level 3 supervisor has probably developed expertise in specific domains, which could be another variable useful in matching supervisees with supervisors.

Level 3 Integrated. Again, this level represents integration across domains. Supervisors at this level are often referred to as "master supervisors." What differentiates them from Level 3 supervisors is that they can work equally well with supervisees at any level, and rarely have definitive preferences. They are especially helpful to both Level 2 supervisees and supervisors. In many agencies with which we are familiar, these supervisors are thought of as "supervisors' supervisors" and are asked to provide supervision to less experienced supervisors. They are noted for their integration of ideas and skills, as is the Level 3 Integrated counselor. One new doctoral level supervisor said of her own Level 3 Integrated supervisor, "I can't believe how quickly and easily he sees the parallels between what's happening with us in supervision and what is going on with me and my supervisee."

Needless to say, the Level 3 Integrated supervisor is also a Level 3 Integrated counselor, and this in itself limits the number of such persons. One can only hope that they are well utilized in the settings in which they work.

Assessment

Thus far in our own work, we have assessed supervisors in terms of experience, self-report, and "general feel" of how they talk about supervision. From a clinical practice standpoint, this has worked well for us. It is obviously insufficient for research purposes. In an attempt to move the field toward more rigorous delineation of supervisor competencies, we suggest that the following elements be used to assess the developmental level of supervisors:

1. level of counselor development (see Chapter Seven)
2. supervisory training experiences (both didactic and experiential)
3. experience as a supervisor (both amount and type)
4. functioning in the three structures (motivation, autonomy, awareness) as related to the supervisory role

By using these four elements and the descriptions of the supervisor levels in this chapter, most supervisors or supervisors-to-be will be able to accurately assess their own level. As is true for counselor levels, there is a tendency to be at different levels across domains. In addition, some supervisors vary in level depending on the level of the supervisee with whom they are working. That is, a supervisor who has attained a Level 3 mode of functioning with most supervisees may find himself or herself operating more at Level 2 when confronted with an especially difficult Level 2 trainee.

This self-assessment can aid both supervisors and those who serve as their consultants or supervisors in addressing issues that will allow them to move toward the next level. This, of course, is especially important for Level 1 and Level 2 supervisors in terms of their providing effective supervisory experiences for trainees. The (usually) slow transformation from Level 3 to Level 3 Integrated appears to be a function of both experience and a careful examination of one's own development and further areas for integration.

An example of this assessment process may be helpful. Dr. X has two years of postdoctoral experience and assesses herself as a Level 3 counselor. She has had no training in supervision and has supervised four trainees, one during her internship and three as a staff member. All were Level 1 trainees except the third, who was clearly at Level 2. Dr. X can recall examples from her experiences that place her at Level 1 during her first experience as a supervisor. She views herself as mostly at Level 2 with her second supervisee. This was especially true in terms of motivation as she was conflicted regarding the importance of the supervisory role. She worked through this with her third supervisee, partly through the use of cognitive interventions with her trainee that were helpful to her as well. In addition, her own supervisor was adept at pointing out parallel processes between Dr. X's reactions and those of her trainee. The supervisor also introduced Dr. X to relevant supervision literature and models, which provided for her a better grasp of the role she was assuming. By the time she started working with her fourth supervisee, Dr. X felt tentatively established at Level 3. She was more consistently motivated, aware of both her supervisee's and her own processes, and able to carry out most supervisory functions in an autonomous manner. Her focus now is on specific tasks, such as learning and using more interventions to help trainees make the transition to Level 2. She also wants to supervise a Level 3 trainee.

Training

As noted earlier in this chapter, practice lags far behind theory in terms of training for supervision. Most beginning supervisors offer trainees a supervisory experience very much like the one that is currently working best for them. Usually this means that they offer a Level 2 or Level 3 supervisory environment to a Level 1 trainee. While this situation offers great learning experiences for the supervisor, it is not helpful (and is sometimes disastrous) for the trainee. Such an approach also raises serious ethical issues (see Chapter Ten). In what other professional area would we allow trainees or professionals to practice without training?

The model of training we propose has two essential components: a conceptual/didactic component and an experiential component. As counselor skills are practiced preceding actual work with clients, we advocate both work on supervision models and constructs and practice prior to the initial supervisory experience. We also offer suggestions on how this training can be done on an in-service basis.

The conceptual component introduces trainees to models and issues in supervision. A diverse pool of readings and lecture and discussion topics are available. We believe that a solid foundation includes at least parts of Kell and Mueller (1966), Ekstein and Wallerstein (1972), Hess (1980), two special issues of *The Counseling Psychologist* (Whiteley, 1982 and 1983), and Russell, Crimmings, and Lent (1984). We hope this book will also be of value. Whatever view is held by the instructor, it is important that students gain a broad look at models available. In terms of issues, we see supervision ethics (see Chapter Ten) and issues related to gender and culture as essential.

We recommend a training approach that includes opportunities to learn and practice supervision skills. Experiential training methods used with basic counseling skills (for example, Ivey, 1971; Kagan and Krathwohl, 1967) can be adapted for use in supervisory training. As with beginning counselors, a crucial activity is acting out the role of the supervisor in any simulation exercise.

As noted earlier, there are a number of training approaches available, most of which offer at least some conceptual and some experiential training (for example, Bernard, 1979; Boyd, 1978). However, none of the training models with which we are familiar offer sufficient depth in conceptual models and issues, and additional resources (such as those listed above) are needed.

In our own training work, we have started relating supervisor level to the format and content of the training. Students who take a course in supervision early in their professional training are labeled "pre-Level 1," in that the role of supervisor is still distant and not a major focus. They are immersed in the tasks of learning how to be an effective counselor and, to that end, how to learn in their role as supervisee. For these students, an introduction to models and issues in the supervision literature is helpful because such exposure allows them some distance to better conceptualize their own experiences and development. It is this group that has provided the most support for the existence of Counselor Level 2 in our model, validating the level with numerous anecdotes. They find it valuable to validate their own experience of the confusion characteristic of Level 2. On the whole, they also find discussions of issues related to ethics and settings helpful.

On the other hand, advanced students and professionals who are just starting to supervise demonstrate the characteristics of a Level 1 supervisor. Their high motivation and their anxiety make them eager for less theory and more experiential learning, with a focus on techniques. Simulation, role playing, and discussion are especially helpful here. Readings that focus on specific methods and techniques are most helpful.

For Level 2 supervisors, their own reactions and commitment to the supervision process are paramount. Training is usually done in groups, and these supervisors usually appear in small numbers in each group. They often require more focus and time to process their own reactions. If they have not already been introduced to basic literature in supervision, most welcome this opportunity.

Given the value both of conceptual and experiential training and different foci for different levels, a series of educational experiences makes the most sense. Professional training programs could offer a conceptually focused academic class to students fairly early in their training. An experientially based pre-supervisory class could be offered late in training or perhaps in conjunction with internship training. This experience could also be packaged as an intensive skill-based workshop, allowing it to be offered on a more flexible schedule. Organizations and agencies could provide workshops or ongoing groups to meet the needs of Level 2 and Level 3 supervisors.

The heart of much learning for the supervisor remains, of course, the supervisory process with his or her own individual supervisor. Assuming the supervisor is at a level appropriate for his or her supervisory task, the prescriptions follow the course for training described above. "Supervisors of supervisors" clearly need to be at our Supervisor Level 3 in order to meet the needs of their own supervisees plus contend with the issues the supervisees raise in regard to their own trainees. This role is excellent for Level 3 Integrated supervisors because they have the skills to deal with two complex layers of supervisory practice— and not forget the client in the process.

Adjunctive Supervisory Modes

Thus far, we have focused on pre-supervision structured learning experiences (for example, classes, workshops) and individual supervision of supervisors. We see these as the core elements in the development of effective supervisors. However, exploration of adjunctive forms merits attention. We view groups and peer supervision as the most viable of such approaches in aiding supervisors to learn individual counseling and therapy. Variations of these approaches have been recommended for teaching and supervising group therapy (Dies, 1980), marriage and family therapy (Everett, 1980), and crisis work (Burkhart, 1980). We focus here on group and peer supervision in the development of effective clinical work with individual clients.

Group Supervision. The use of a group format for supervision of counselor trainees is a frequent practice, as noted by Holloway and Johnson (1985). In fact, such an approach is specified both by the American Personnel and Guidance Association (currently the American Association of Counseling and Development) for practicum sites (1977) and by the American Psychological Association's criteria for accreditation for internship training (1979).

Little theoretical or empirical work in this area has appeared in recent years. However, Holloway and Johnson (1985) have published a helpful review of group supervision, defined as a format in which a supervisor oversees a trainee's professional development in a group of peers. Holloway and Johnson note that interpersonal process groups were prevalent during the 1960s and early 1970s. Today, a case presentation approach is commonly used. This approach usually involves case presentations, of course, as well as attention to both didactic material and group dynamics (Orton, 1965; Fraleigh and Buchheimer, 1969; Rioch, Coulter, and Weinberger, 1976). Rioch, Coulter, and Weinberger have presented a comprehensive model that allows trainees to struggle with their own issues as well as client dynamics but that keeps the focus on the professional context.

Sansbury (1982) advocates a developmental framework

for group supervision, viewing this format as a strategy for teaching counseling skills with attendant growth in interpersonal awareness. Sansbury's model of supervision includes four areas to which the supervisor should attend (p. 54):

1. teaching interventions directed at the entire group;
2. specific case-oriented information, suggestions, or feedback;
3. affective responses of a particular supervisee as the feelings pertain to his or her client, and;
4. the group's interaction and development, which can be used to facilitate supervisee exploration, openness, and responsibility.

All the above are relevant for the group supervision approach. It is our experience that the level of the trainees determines which areas receive most attention. More structured interventions by the leader are needed by Level 1 trainees. Level 2 trainees, given an environment of trust, are apt to focus on affective responses and their own fluctuating motivation. They also are likely to challenge the trainers' conceptualization of client issues (assuming they feel safe in so doing). Level 3 trainees often want to use group supervision time to try out their ideas regarding client conceptualizations and interventions.

Our own view is that the models of Sansbury and others are best used in a mixed group of Level 1, Level 2, and beginning Level 3 trainees. The modeling done by more advanced (Level 3) trainees is reassuring to both Level 1 and Level 2 trainees and provides a balance for the disruption in the group engendered by Level 2 counselors. We have found it very useful to share our developmental model in group supervision because it legitimizes each level as valid and important. This appears to be especially essential for Level 2 trainees.

The main difficulty with group supervision, of course, is how to meet the diverse needs of trainees both at different levels and with individual issues and concerns. It is all too easy to retreat to a highly structured format (which works for Level 1 trainees but does not encourage them to move on) or to use group processes exclusively (which works best for Level 3 trainees). A mix, suggested also by Sansbury and others, seems essential to us. While not every intervention is appropriate for each trainee, such an approach gives counselors a more complete understanding of the process of counselor development and allows for the peer support and challenge so necessary for growth.

Of course, we assume that the trainer or leader in group supervision is functioning at an appropriate level of supervisor development (Level 3 or Level 3 Integrated). In support of this statement, we note that Pierce and Schauble (1971) found that as long as a supervisee had one high level supervisor—whether an individual or group supervisor—he or she demonstrated improvement in facilitative conditions.

There are clear ethical issues involved in group supervision (see Chapter Ten). In addition, there is no substantive empirical research on current models. Holloway and Johnson (1985) call for a systematic examination of the group supervision process, with attention to goals, format, and evaluation. We agree with their statement that "without a systematic effort of this nature, group supervision will remain a weak link in our training programs, widely practiced and poorly justified" (p. 12).

Peer Supervision. This approach—which assumes some equality of colleagues—can be used either in a group or a dyadic setting, on a regular or as-needed basis. Clearly, group supervision also offers an opportunity for modeling and input by peers. Peer supervision seems to be used mostly by professionals at an advanced stage, either in combination with individual supervision or as a sole source of supervision. For many of us, the opportunity to use a peer to work through difficult clinical problems and to provide support and challenge is a highly rewarding professional experience. At later stages, a peer supervisor is someone we chose, and the process is outside the formal evaluation process. Our peers are (ideally) working with a set of client and personal issues similar to ours and can thus understand our own concerns. Moreover, even peers who are very similar in terms of counselor development often have different perspectives, interests, and expertise.

While the use of peers seems to be helpful at earlier stages, we see this format as especially useful in producing the changes necessary to move from Level 3 to Level 3 Integrated. In fact, since we believe that this transition is usually made by professionals who are no longer receiving regular one-to-one supervision, the opportunity to work closely with a peer or group of peers may be largely responsible for movement to Level 3 Integrated.

We do not, of course, discount the possibility that one-to-one supervision for many Level 3 supervisees incorporates many of the aspects and values of peer supervision. The crucial difference is that in peer supervision both (or all) participants are responsible for sharing and discussing issues. Thus, whether experienced early or late in the development process, peer supervision allows the counselor to move beyond his or her own issues and attend to another in a unique way. One young professional, speaking of this process, stated, "It made me less selfish, somehow. As a counselor, I know I need to attend to my client. But to forget my own issues and really try to help a colleague—well, that gave me a new dimension on what being a professional is all about." Peer supervision, then, provides additional dimensions to both the counselor and supervisor role and allows achievement of a fully collegial stance in trainees and professionals alike.

Next Steps in Research

Russell, Crimmings, and Lent (1984, p. 671) advise researchers to determine "what training or supervision methods administered by what types of supervisor are most effective for which types of supervisee on what criteria." They note that developmental models are an especially promising line of research because these models assume that certain methods are useful for supervisees at certain stages.

One way to begin such a research program is to assess the level of the supervisor, use the appropriate training and/or supervision, and evaluate the results. Evaluation is probably the most difficult point here because the perceptions of both the supervisor and the supervisee are valid, as are those of the person being supervised by the trainee. We hope that progress continues toward more objective assessment of supervisor development so that it can be included in evaluation as well.

Our assumptions regarding appropriate training by levels need also to be tested by comparing our training focus with more generalized training. So far, only our clinical sense and trainee comments support us in these assertions.

Assessment of trainer or supervisor level is yet another variable that should make a difference, based on assumptions in the developmental literature plus the research cited earlier in this chapter.

Level 2 supervisors remain a bit of a puzzle. Our impression, stated earlier, is that supervisors either negotiate this level quickly or opt out of the supervisory role. In any case, we have worked with very few Level 2 supervisors; a better understanding of this level and appropriate interventions is needed. It may be that there are more Level 2 supervisors than we are aware of because they share with Level 2 trainees a reluctance to admit to conflicts and confusion. Or, alternatively, there may not be a valid, structurally relevant Level 2 for supervisors, at least in the way it has been described here.

Further research is definitely needed on instruments to measure supervisor development. Work is also required to further delineate and specify appropriate training and supervisory environments.

Use of a developmental approach implies that research will also attend to appropriate person variables such as gender, ethnicity, and experience. We need to clarify how these and other possibly relevant variables interact with both supervisor level and effectiveness in the supervisory role.

Perhaps more than anything else, we see a strong need for longitudinal studies of trainees from the time they begin professional training through several years of postdoctoral work. This can help validate (or refute) our developmental model, both for counselors and supervisors. In addition, it should provide the information needed to develop effective training and supervisory environments. If supervision is to become an integrated, viable professional role, such work is essential.

10

Ethical and Other Issues:

Implications for Research and Practice

In this final chapter, we attempt to add both specificity and breadth to our ideas regarding supervision. First, we explore two areas of critical importance in the practice of supervision: ethics and law. To the extent feasible, we take a developmental perspective in addressing these two areas. We then turn to a further exploration of some issues touched on in earlier chapters—those concerning gender and ethnicity. In the last part of the chapter, we sum up our views on developmental models of supervision and discuss our hopes and visions of what needs to be done over the next few years in the supervision area, both in practice and in research.

Ethical Considerations

Newman (1981) proposed three major reasons for an examination of ethical issues in clinical supervision: (1) supervision serves as the primary training mode for teaching skills in counseling and therapy; (2) the supervisory relationship is one of inherently unequal status, power, and expertise; and (3) the relationship possesses therapy-like qualities, insofar as self-evaluation and expectations of personal growth are concerned. Other authors (Cormier and Bernard, 1982; Schmidt and Meara,

1984) have also called attention to the importance of ethics in the context of supervision.

Ethical principles relating to supervision can be viewed in three ways. The first encompasses general principles of ethical conduct articulated by ethicists. The second is ethical codes, binding on all professionals and professionals-in-training, developed by each profession (for example, psychology, social work). A third way to discuss principles is in terms that directly address the supervisor and the supervisory relationship. We will limit our discussion to ethical codes and principles that are directly relevant to the supervisory function. This literature is scarce, but key provisions are worth noting.

The "Ethical Principles of Psychologists" of the American Psychological Association (1981, p. 636) includes two sections that refer directly to the supervisory function. Principle 6a proposes that "psychologists make every effort to avoid dual relationships that could impair their professional judgment or increase the risk of exploitation. Examples of such dual relationships include, but are not limited to, research with and treatment of employees, students, supervisees, close friends, or relatives." Principle 7d suggests that "psychologists do not exploit their professional relationships with supervisees, students, employees, or research participants sexually or otherwise." Two other sections refer indirectly to supervision. Principle 5a states that "information obtained in clinical or consulting relationships, or evaluative data concerning children, students, employees, and others is discussed only for professional purposes and only with persons clearly concerned with the case." Principle 2 states that psychologists "only provide services and use techniques for which they are qualified by training and experience" (1981, p. 634). These statements, taken together, prohibit many dual relationships and exploitation, protect appropriate confidentiality in the supervisory relationship, and mandate supervisory competence. Unfortunately, they do not address some of the more specific and complex ethical issues that arise in supervision.

The ethical codes of both the American College Personnel Association (Canon and Brown, 1985) and the North Atlantic Association for Counselor Education and Supervision (Hart,

1982) speak to the responsibility of professional members to assess trainees in terms of professional competencies and personal limitations, to assist trainees in securing assistance, and to screen out those students who are unable to work effectively as professionals. The latter document also includes a statement that "counselor educators and supervisors should have the same respect for their trainees as counselors have for their counselees" (1982, p. 245). In addition, the document states that "expectations should be made clear. Allowances should be made for freedom of choice. Under no circumstances should counselor educators and supervisors attempt to sway trainees to adopt a particular theoretical belief or point of view" (p. 245).

In "Standards for Providers of Psychological Services," the American Psychological Association (1977) specifies that individuals who do not meet the requirements for the designation of "professional psychologist" shall be "supervised by a professional psychologist who shall assume professional responsibility and accountability for the services provided.

A number of recommended guidelines for supervisory practice have emerged. Most notable is an American Psychological Association document that suggests standards of competency for supervisors. The paper, written by the Division of Psychotherapy (1971), includes a statement that "the faculty (of training programs) should be competent in the supervision aspect of teaching psychotherapy" (p. 151).

Little research in the area of ethics and clinical supervision has appeared. Perhaps the most relevant (and alarming!) is a study by Pope, Levenson, and Schover (1979) that indicated that 10 percent of a sample of therapists (3 percent of males and almost 17 percent of the females) reported sexual contact as a student with at least one of their psychology educators (including supervisors). In 1980, Pope, Schover, and Levenson published an article discussing the implications of sexual behavior between clinical supervisors and trainees for professional standards.

Both Newman (1981) and Cormier and Bernard (1982) have examined ethical issues in supervision and made recommendations. Based on this literature, the codes, and our own thinking, we identify four clusters of issues crucial for ethical supervision.

Competency. Principle 2 of the American Psychological Association (1981) ethics discusses the necessity of high standards of competence for all psychologists and mandates provision only of services for which psychologists are trained. Given the current lack of training in supervision (see Chapter Eight), there appears to be a serious ethical issue in regard to competency to supervise. Just as we now consider it unethical to counsel without prior training, we may soon apply the same idea to supervision. A requirement for competent practice is supervisor awareness of models of supervision and research support for such models. Given the explosion in this area (see Chapter Two) during the past decade, this is no easy task. Nevertheless, it is necessary for ethical practice.

In terms of competency for use of our model, a minimum would be the self-training available through reading, consulting, and perhaps attendance at relevant in-service training. At the very least, the supervisor should be aware of his or her limitations and avoid the mismatches described in Chapter Eight.

Dual Relationships. This is an especially difficult area in the practice of supervision. Sexual relationships with current or former supervisees can be avoided, as can counseling relationships or use of the supervisee as a research participant. More of a problem, we believe, is the situation in which the supervisor or potential supervisor is a member of the supervisee's program faculty or the employer of the supervisee. A number of programs prefer to have trainees supervised by their own faculty. And there are certainly numerous situations in which a faculty member, advisor, or an employer is the supervisor most desired by the supervisee or deemed the best match by all concerned. Such situations can and do work and are often the best solutions, especially in small programs and agencies. However, such relationships should be approached with caution. It is critical that the supervisee have genuine choice in this matter and not be routinely assigned to a faculty member, employer, or other person with whom the student has another authority relationship. In addition, it is important for the supervisor and supervisee to openly discuss the implications of this arrangement at the start of supervision. The experience of one of us with several such situations was that the match was the best available and that it worked well, but that in each case there was some clear and persistent anxiety on the part of the supervisee regarding the relationship.

The same cautions, we believe, should be applied to friendships and general social relationships. These matches should be avoided when possible; if embarked upon, possible ramifications should be openly explored.

Respect for Supervisees. This is a somewhat catchall cluster that includes confidentiality, appropriate supervisory methods, open and fair evaluation processes, and clarity regarding expectations. Good practice, we think, mandates consistent attention to these variables throughout the supervisory relationship. Respect for diversity, in terms of individual differences among trainees, is also essential. In the area of confidentiality, the supervisor should be explicit regarding what information about the supervisee she or he will share, with whom, and with what process. While aspects of supervision are almost always shared beyond the supervisory dyad, this should be clarified for the supervisee.

The Supervisee's Ethics. This is a topic rarely formally (but often informally) discussed. Given the inherent inequality of the relationship, most attention is, and should be, focused on the ethics of the supervisor. Nonetheless, trainees are also held accountable to professional ethics, and those relevant to their role as supervisees merit consideration. Principle 2f of the American Psychological Association (1981) code mandates that psychologists recognize personal problems that may interfere with effectiveness and that they seek competent assistance. In our experience, this can be a difficult area for trainees, and one that is sometimes avoided. Supervisees who are aware of their own problems should seriously consider their clinical supervisors as primary sources of assistance and, if appropriate, for referrals for personal counseling. If trainees choose to work with another professional, it is important to at least let the supervisor know that there is a problem. The supervisor's ethical and legal responsibility for services provided by the supervisee (see next section) requires that at least minimal, relevant information be shared with the supervisor.

Supervisees also owe respect and consideration to the supervisor. If difficulties prevent a mutually respectful relationship, supervisees need first to seek help in improving the relationship and then, if unsuccessful, to seek appropriate consultation in finding a better supervisory setting. The situation should be treated as a confidential one and discussed only with a limited number of appropriate mentors and peers. Too often, a frustrated supervisee gossips about a supervisor rather than using positive and ethical approaches to either improve the situation or leave it. Given current limited training for the supervisory role, it is not surprising that supervisees encounter problems of incompetence, as well as the expected and useful difficulties inherent in an effective supervisory process. Such difficulties require expert assessment and consultation, and supervisees are urged to expend every effort to procure such assistance.

Legal Considerations

Legal issues in supervision have been discussed in the literature, notably by Slovenko (1980) and Cormier and Bernard (1982). Probably the most important motivation for this topic is the growing demand for accountability in all segments of professional practice. Thus the extent of a supervisor's responsibility for a supervisee's practice is an issue of growing interest and importance. This issue goes right to the heart of the ethical injunction (discussed in this chapter) against imposing a theoretical bias on supervisees and also to the appropriate movement toward autonomy explicit in our developmental model. Three arenas—ethics, competent practice, and law—must play a part in the resolution of any specific issue of supervisory responsibility.

Legal responsibility of supervisors is most clearly delineated in statutes of the states that regulate the independent practice of the profession. As Slovenko (1980) notes, psychotherapy has been the subject of few malpractice suits. Most of the suits filed have centered on ethical violations and, more recently, on issues of failure to disclose relevant information or gain informed consent. Slovenko (1980, p. 462) notes that "the psychotherapy supervisor assumes, in general, clinical responsibility much as if the patient were under his (or her) own personal care." Thus stated, it is clear that a heavy responsibility accompanies the supervisory role. Slovenko illustrates several potential areas of malpractice in which the supervisor might be held liable. These include situations such as the trainee (even with the supervisor's help) being incapable of offering proper therapy or a client consenting to treatment without knowing that the service will be offered by a trainee.

Dawidoff (1973) notes that supervisors may also be liable if treatment (by the supervisee) is terminated or a referral made without due cause. Van Hoose and Kottler (1985) point out that failure to adequately supervise a counselor who is treating a disturbed client is a leading complaint of current malpractice suits.

A legal problem—in addition to the compelling ethical ones—with dual relationships is that they can provide the basis for an allegation of failure to provide adequate supervision in a lawsuit (Cormier and Bernard, 1982). Failure to warn a potential victim, as illustrated in the well-known case of Tarasoff v. the Regents of the University of California, is another supervisory legal issue often cited (for example, Cormier and Bernard, 1982; Slovenko, 1980). In this case, the California Supreme Court ruled that a psychotherapist who has reason to believe that a patient may injure or kill another must notify the potential victim, his or her relatives, or the authorities. Slovenko (1980), in his discussion of this case, notes a statement by the attorney for Tarasoff to the effect that if the supervisor had personally examined the patient and made a decision that the patient was not dangerous, there would possibly have been no case.

What then is the best course of action for the prudent supervisor? We recommend a close study of the work of Cormier and Bernard (1982) and Slovenko (1980). Cormier and Bernard suggest that supervision be scheduled on the basis of a careful assessment of the needs of both client and supervisee and that it be carefully documented. It may be advisable for the supervisor to make an independent assessment of very disturbed or possibly dangerous clients being seen by the supervisee. Certainly, the best policy is to follow any relevant laws as well as generally accepted good practice.

Most important, it is vital that the supervisor be well trained, knowledgeable, and skilled in the practice of clinical supervision. The supervisor should be cognizant of crucial legal issues and should examine his or her work with these questions in mind.

Assuming the importance then of ethical and legal issues for supervisors, what can we say about training models in this regard? Clearly, effective supervision can be practiced ethically and legally from a diversity of models or constructs. The crucial components are knowledge and serious consideration of ethical and legal issues. We believe that a number of elements in our developmental model enhance ethical and legal practice.

For example, our focus on assessment draws attention to a number of variables—including supervisor, supervisee, and setting—crucial for competency and sound practice. Inclusion of setting considerations in the model allows a focus on constraints and opportunities for competent practice and draws attention to system components that may mitigate against sound and ethical practice. The inclusion of levels, domains, and specified interventions highlights the consistency necessary for good practice and underlines key issues for supervisory decision making. The focus on training helps to ensure that supervisors attain a reasonable level of competency in their work with specific attention paid to ethical and legal issues.

Gender and Ethnicity

Several times in this book, we have alluded to ways in which individual differences, gender in particular, may influence supervisee development. For example, we noted that at Level 2 females may be more prone than males to overidentify with

client affect, while males may avoid affect and offer inappropriate cognitive interventions. At this point an extended look at
the domain of individual differences is warranted. We cannot
adequately cover all the differences found among our trainees,
such as age, socioeconomic status, and sexual orientation. Instead, we focus on gender and ethnicity and hope that our approach can be expanded by the reader.

In recent years there has been increasing attention to gender and ethnic differences in development. Gilligan (1982) asserts that women's moral development is centered around
understanding responsibility and relationships in context, or
the "ethics of care." She notes that the conception of morality
as fairness, which ties moral development to the understanding
of rights and rules, is more typical of males. Benack (1982) describes a tendency toward "relativistic" thinking in the development of many women. Payton (1985) speaks of the barriers to
development, engendered by sexism and racism, for ethnic minority women.

Levine and Padilla (1980) cite research suggesting that
when individuals of an ethnic minority reject their heritage,
they tend to exhibit self-derogation, psychosomatic sympto-
matology, personal guilt, anxiety, and fear. Bicultural or multicultural identifications are seen as producing academic and personal success and stability (Sue, 1981). The development of
bicultural or multicultural identity is outlined by a number of
writers in the professional literature, including Sue (1981) and
Smith (1985).

It seems therefore that any model of supervision must be
judged partly on how it treats the development of women and
ethnic minorities. As Vasquez and McKinley (1982, p. 60) assert, "if we are to promote maximum growth in minority supervisees, we must attend to and stimulate their efforts to incorporate ethnic identity with professional identity." Let us turn to a
discussion of how our model may be useful in that enterprise.

First, we need to be aware of possible gender and ethnic
differences in supervisee development and to explore these in
both clinical practice and research. We have noted from our
practice the tendency of women at Level 2 to overidentify with

the client and perhaps wallow in confusion, while men may attempt to escape the necessary ambivalence this level requires by focusing primarily on cognition. Our model suggests close attention to these possible differences, with perhaps more cognitive interventions for women and more affective ones for men at Level 2. The overall tone of support in supervision may be more crucial for women, who tend to respond positively to the nurturance of the environment. Given findings (Marecek and Johnson, 1980) that women tend to be more focused on relationships and men more focused on tasks, it may be that females will bond more in supervisory dyads. However, Worthington and Stern (1985) report that both male supervisees and supervisors thought they had a better relationship with their partner (supervisor or supervisee), regardless of gender, than did female supervisees. Supervisees overall felt they had a closer relationship with same-gender supervisors.

Our clinical experience thus far in using the model is that same-gender pairings are particularly fruitful for exploring the domains of individual differences and professional ethics. Cross-gender pairings, especially at Level 2, may best help trainees to see a different view of clients and their issues.

There is another arena—that of termination—in which we see gender issues as crucial. Termination of supervision, as is true of termination of clients, is an important topic in the literature (for example, Kell and Mueller, 1966). In our practice, we see gender differences well described by the relationship focus for females articulated by Gilligan (1982). That is, females often experience difficulty "saying good-bye" and males may have problems "saying hello." All counselors need to understand this in regard to clients. Supervisors, in addition, must be sensitive to the reality that, for at least some proportion of our female supervisees, this is a very difficult issue. For female supervisors with female supervisees, the danger is that the crucial "good-bye" may not be said, leaving both participants in a sort of limbo regarding their relationship and the work they did together. For male trainees, the "good-bye" may come too easily, thus creating a pseudo termination in which affect is suppressed rather than acknowledged.

We have also noted different termination issues for supervisees at various developmental levels, regardless of gender. Level 1 supervisees are often initially reluctant to terminate and give up a mentor. However, once the transition is made, they tend to bond quickly with a new supervisor. Level 2 trainees, if they felt supported by the supervisor, show skepticism toward the new supervisor. If supervision has been turbulent, there is usually relief and a perceived opportunity to hide. At Level 3, termination is much like a bittersweet parting of friends.

Vasquez and McKinley (1982) examine the development of a bicultural identity using the Loganbill, Hardy, and Delworth (1982) model. They describe an ethnic minority supervisee at each level, and deal with issues such as competition and articulation. For example, they point out that the ethnic minority counselor at Level 2 may find herself or himself trying to decide where to apply her or his skills. "Many minority professionals," they write, "experience internal and external pressures to return to one's community and 'work in the trenches' " (p. 61). Sue's (1981) model of minority identity development includes four stages that work well with our developmental model, moving from unawareness of the minority culture to establishment of a bicultural identity.

Ivey (1986, p. 320) states that "empathy demands awareness of both the individual and the culture." If therapists must possess this ability, supervisors must to an even greater degree. For as supervisors, we are responsible not only for trainees but for their clients as well. In our practice, we have seen several instances in which supervisor deficiencies in these areas led to ethical problems for trainees and clients. Often, more recently trained therapists, perhaps themselves women or members of ethnic minorities, provide challenges in these areas to their supervisors.

Ethical counselors must be aware of current models and thinking in the discipline. Cross-cultural counseling competencies are crucial, and Division 17 (Counseling) of the American Psychological Association (Sue and others, 1982) and the Task Force on Sex Bias and Sex Role Stereotyping in Psychotherapeutic Practice (1978) have provided valuable guidelines for those working with members of ethnic minorities and women, whether as clients or as supervisees. We advise supervisors to study these guidelines and to use either our model or another to maximize the relevant contributions of gender and ethnicity.

Hopes and Visions

We come at last to some final caveats, to some hopes and visions for the next few years in the arena of practice and research in supervision. Development, we stated in Chapter One, is but a metaphor for some process about which we know something but not enough. As Ivey (1986, p. 3) states, "the journey is development; the destination is an inevitable repetition of our return to where we began (but with a new state of awareness)."

We believe that supervision is a crucial process in the training of therapists and counselors. As such, the supervisory process merits much more attention in terms of theory, research, and thoughtful practice than it has been given. Russell, Crimmings, and Lent (1984, p. 675) state that "the recent trend toward developmental conceptions of supervisee growth may be a step" toward clear, explicit theoretical statements regarding supervision. We hope and believe we have made at least one step in that direction with our model.

At this point, we urge our practitioner readers, both supervisors and supervisees, to think seriously about the model in terms of their own experience and work. Beyond that, there is a need, perhaps even an ethical imperative, for training programs and service settings to offer education discussing both what we know about supervision and what we need to know. If we agree on the necessity of training for the role of counselor, perhaps we are ready to admit that such training is needed for the supervisory role as well.

Developmental models of supervision are new and largely based on practice. There is a crucial need for research on their efficacy and utility. So far, the models have received some general support in the research literature, but there has been limited testing of specific hypotheses. For example, is our Level 2 not found in research because it is not there or because we have not used the appropriate methods to discover it? As developmental models become more elegant, as we hope this one has, and researchers become more creative in devising tests, we will see better tests of the validity and utility of these models.

Russell, Crimmings, and Lent (1984) present a multilevel model for organizing supervision research that includes both process and outcome variables. Their model is worth serious consideration. We would add to it a study of the settings in which supervision and counseling occur, since we remain convinced that the context of supervision is one factor in successful outcomes.

Development, as we understand it, involves moving up, moving outward, and moving inward. Our model, as others, must be tested for its ability to explain, facilitate, and predict this process in supervision. Supervision demands scientific rigor but also art and commitment to the enterprise. We apply to supervision Whitehead's (1950, pp. 370-371) wise thoughts regarding education: "The paradox which wrecks so many promising theories of education is that the training which produces skill is so very apt to stifle imaginative zest. Skill demands repetition, and imaginative zest is tinged with impulse. Up to a certain point each skill opens new paths for the imagination. But in each individual, formal training has its limit of usefulness."

THE FINAL SUPERVISION

When the board was set for play,
There was the chessmaster and the pawn.

"What is it you wish of me?" queried the chessmaster.
"To help me to become a knight," answered the pawn.
"And why are you not already what you wish?" asked the
        chessmaster.
"I have no armor, no sword, and no horse," said the pawn.
"And you wish that I should provide that for you!" demanded the
        chessmaster.
"Oh, no, not that," replied the faltering pawn. "I wish only
        that you show me the means by which they may be acquired."
"Agreed," responded the chessmaster.

And the game was begun.

"Why do you move up and not down?" challenged the chessmaster.
        Why do you move right and not left?"
"Because down brings pain, and right brings fear and
        uncertainty," the pawn responded defensively.
"Ah yes," replied the chessmaster, "that is most true."
"But down and to the right—that is where the armor lies."
So the pawn stiffened resolutely and then moved down and to the
        right.
And there was the suit of armor.
The pawn concealed the feeling of victory.

The chessmaster pressed for the next move.

"Your moves are calculated and so predictable," commented the
        chessmaster. "You are too easily placed in check."
"But that is the way of the game," pleaded the pawn. "One must
        calculate in order to continue to move."
"That is so," replied the chessmaster. "But that is not the way
        of the true knower. The testing of limitations—that is
        where the sweet pleasure of victory lies."
The pawn was frightened, but responded by boldly placing the
        chessmaster in check.
The chessmaster disguised delight and chose instead to swiftly
        check the pawn to force yet another maneuver.
The pawn escaped and chose to move again, and again, and yet
        again.
"Aha," commended the sullen chessmaster. "I see you have
        acquired a sword."

And the chessmaster again forced the pawn into check.

181

The pawn grew tired with the movement and the burden of its
    tools.
"I now have armor and a sword," stated the pawn, "but my moves
    are awkward and confining. I need a horse."
"The horse will be yours when it is," replied the chessmaster.
So, with each attempt, the armor was donned and the sword was
    polished and ground to precision.
The armor slowly lost its bulk and burden, and the sword was
    manipulated with direction and expectancy.
"Perhaps I no longer need a horse to become a knight," offered
    the pawn. And the horse appeared.
"Because you no longer demand expediency in your moves, they may
    now be yours," said the chessmaster.

And the chessmaster turned away and smiled.

"I am beginning to feel much like a knight," stated the pawn,
    speculatively. "Will my time come soon?"
"What will be the signs by which you judge your knighthood?"
    questioned the chessmaster.
"I will be both sparse and generous, both dubious and sure, both
    right and left, both stern and yielding, both up and down,
    both young and old," answered the pawn.
"And what is it that you are now?" followed the chessmaster.
"I feel that I am that," replied the pawn.
"Yes," responded the chessmaster. "I see that you are."
"Would you tell me then that, because I have the feelings of a
    knight, I have now become as one?" queried the excited pawn.
"No," answered the chessmaster. "That is not the nature of the
    movement. Knighthood has always been within the pawn. And
    in your acceptance of what lies within and in your
    acknowledgment of the responsibility of your movement, you
    have become as I."

And the game began anew.
    As the board was laid,
    There were two chessmasters.

Karen A. Pirnot
University of Iowa

Resource A

Instruments for Assessing
Supervisors and Trainees

The following table lists instruments that have been used in previous supervision research. It is followed by brief descriptions of each of the instruments. This information is referred to in the Chapter Seven discussion of assessment in supervision. These instruments are useful both for research and practice in clinical supervision.

Table R-1. Instruments for Assessment in Supervision.

Evaluator	Focal Person	Context of Evaluation	Instrument
Supervisor	Supervisor	Supervision Sessions	LSS DLDS E-Scale SSI-S SPF-S SQ
Supervisor	Trainee	Supervision Sessions	OMART SLQ-S SNQ-S DLDS P-Scale
Supervisor	Trainee	Counseling Sessions	OMART SLQ-S DLDS P-Scale

(continued on next page)

Table R-1. Instruments for Assessment in Supervision, Cont'd.

Evaluator	Focal Person	Context of Evaluation	Instrument
Trainee	Supervisor	Supervision Sessions	SQ SC CDQ SPF-T CIQ SSI-T
Trainee	Trainee	Supervision Sessions	SLQ-T SNQ-T CDQ SPF-T CIQ SC
Trainee	Trainee	Counseling Sessions	SLQ-T CDQ CIQ SC
Client	Trainee	Counseling Sessions	CRF CEI CARS
Observer	Supervisor	Supervision Sessions	BIA NCS SQ SC SSI-T DLDS E-Scale
Observer	Trainee	Supervision Sessions	BIA OMART DLDS P-Scale SLQ-S
Observer	Trainee	Counseling Sessions	OMART SLQ-S DLDS P-Scale

Note: Format adapted from Holloway (1984).

LSS. Level of Supervision Survey (Miars and others, 1983). Assesses dimensions of the supervision process. Most items constructed to tap supervision environments postulated by Stoltenberg (1981). Five sections with sixty-five 5-point Likert-type items: perceptions of importance of aspects of supervision, frequency of in-session behaviors, time spent in various supervisory functions, presence of supervisor roles and behaviors, and demographic variables describing the supervisor.

DLDS E-Scale. Developmental Level Determination Scale, Environment Scale (Wiley, 1982). Supervisor questionnaire with twenty Likert items addressing characteristics of supervision environments for each of the four trainee developmental levels postulated by Stoltenberg (1981). Items include five aspects of the supervision environment: role of supervisor, affective focus of supervision, cognitive and skills focus of supervision, dependency in supervision, and role of support and confrontation.

DLDS P-Scale. Developmental Level Determination Scale, Person Scale (Wiley, 1982). Supervisor questionnaire with twenty Likert items about characteristics of trainees for each of the four trainee developmental levels postulated by Stoltenberg (1981). Items address five areas of development: degree of confidence in present counseling skill, insight about impact on clients, approach to a theoretical framework, sense of professional identity, and awareness of limitation of counseling.

SSI-S, SSI-T. Supervisory Styles Inventory (Friedlander and Ward, 1984). Parallel questionnaires for supervisors and trainees with twenty-five 7-point Likert items (plus eight filler items) representing three scales describing supervisor styles: attractive, interpersonally sensitive, and task-oriented. The instrument is based on a conceptual model of interrelated sources of variability among supervisors, of which supervisory style is the primary focus for this assessment device.

SPF-S, SPF-T. Supervisor Perception Form (Heppner and Roehlke, 1984). Parallel questionnaires for supervisors and trainees consisting of twenty-five 6-point Likert items making up two separate scales: supervisory impact and willingness to learn. The Supervisory Impact Scale taps the supervisor's (form

S) and the trainee's (form T) perceptions of the supervisor's impact on various counseling skills for the trainee, including diagnosing and assessment, new counseling techniques, case management, and case conceptualizations. The Willingness to Learn Scale taps supervisor and trainee perceptions of the trainee's openness and receptivity to suggestions by the supervisor.

SQ. Supervision Questionnaire (Worthington and Roehlke, 1979). This instrument consists of forty-two items assessing perceived importance of supervisor behaviors rated on a 5-point Likert scale. Factor analysis yielded two independent factors: evaluation and support. The instrument can be completed by supervisors or trainees.

SLQ-T, SLQ-S. Supervisee Levels Questionnaire (McNeill, Stoltenberg, and Pierce, 1985). This instrument consists of twenty-four 7-point Likert items constructed to examine three dimensions of trainee development based on Stoltenberg's (1981) model of counselor development: dependency-autonomy, self-awareness, and theory and skills. This self-report questionnaire can be answered by trainees (form T) or by supervisors instructed to rate their trainees (form S).

SNQ-T, SNQ-S. Supervisee Needs Questionnaire (Stoltenberg, Pierce, and McNeill, 1987). This self-report questionnaire consists of thirty 7-point Likert items designed to assess perceived needs by trainees for the supervision environment. The instrument contains five scales relevant to trainee needs in the supervision process: structure, instruction, feedback, support and availability, and self-direction. The instrument can be answered by the trainee in terms of his or her own perceived needs in supervision or by the supervisor as he or she perceives the needs of the trainee.

OMART. The Oetting-Michaels Anchored Ratings for Therapists (Michaels, 1982). This instrument is completed by the supervisor and assesses the trainee on thirty-four behaviors and activities related to the counseling and supervision process. Behavioral descriptions of the constructs are recorded by the supervisor, who then rates the trainee on particular dimensions using a continuous scale with descriptive anchors provided at various points. The instrument assesses behaviors relevant to interviewing, conceptualization of therapy, reaction to supervision, and sensitivity to both client and trainee issues.

SC. Supervision Checklist (Rabinowitz, Heppner, and Roehlke, 1985). This self-report questionnaire consists of two parts: a list of twelve critical incidents in the supervision process and seven important supervisor interventions. As a process measure, the trainee is asked to pick the two most important critical incidents dealt with during any given supervision session. In addition, the trainee is asked to choose the most important of the seven categories of interventions made by his or her supervisor during each weekly supervision session. As a supervision outcome measure, the trainee is asked at the end of the term to rate the overall importance of the twelve critical incidents on a 7-point Likert scale. Similarly, the seven supervisor interventions are rated for overall importance at the end of the term.

CIQ. Critical Incidents Questionnaire (Heppner and Roehlke, 1984). This is an open-ended questionnaire completed by the trainee that asks the trainee to describe incidents in supervision that resulted in changes in the trainee's perceptions of his or her effectiveness as a counselor. Specifically, the trainee is asked to describe the incident(s), explain why it was critically important, and indicate when the incident occurred during the term.

CDQ. Counselor Development Questionnaire (Reising and Daniels, 1983). This trainee self-report questionnaire is designed to address issues related to Hogan's (1964) model of trainee development. The instrument consists of one hundred fifty-seven 5-point Likert items making up two subtests: the Trainee Subtest and the Supervisory Needs Subtest. The questionnaire has additional items about demographic variables and counseling experience. Sixteen factors emerged from factor analysis, eight for each subtest. The trainee factors included anxiety and doubt, independence, commitment ambivalence, method, self-understanding, work validation, criticism readiness, and supervision comfort. The supervisory needs factors were emotional consultation, skills training, mutuality, respectful confrontation, reciprocal confrontation, benign support, behavioral monitoring, and peer consultation.

CRF. Counselor Rating Form (Barak and LaCrosse, 1975). This instrument was designed to measure constructs relevant to Strong's (1968) interpersonal influence process. Three dimensions are included on the scale: counselor expertness, attractiveness, and trustworthiness. Each dimension is described by twelve bipolar items using a 7-point Likert format. The instrument can be completed either by the client or other observers.

CEI. Counselor Evaluation Inventory (Linden, Stone, and Shertzer, 1965). This instrument, a modification of the Interview Rating Scale (Anderson and Anderson, 1962), is intended to get at client-counselor rapport and counselor effectiveness. The scale, usually completed by the client, consists of twenty-one 5-point Likert items addressing three factors: counseling climate, counselor comfort, and client satisfaction.

CARS. Current Adjustment Rating Scale (Truax as described in Berzins, Bedner, and Severy, 1975). This self-report instrument is designed to measure change in the client over the course of counseling or therapy. Seven areas are addressed in terms of a client's current perceived "likeability" and functioning, yielding fourteen items in a 5-point Likert format. The seven areas are work, relationships with friends and family, love relationships, education and school, sexual relationships, leisure time, and an overall rating.

BIA. Blumberg's Interactional Analysis (Holloway, 1982). This system is a modification of Blumberg's (1968) work measuring interpersonal interactions in an educational environment. The revised system consists of sixteen categories coded by observers in 5-second intervals. Ten of the categories describe supervisor behavior, four describe trainee behavior, one codes silence, and the last indicates whether the dyad is listening to an audio- or videotape. The system uses two trained raters. The resulting codings are reorganized into a composite transition frequency matrix that is then subjected to a sequential analysis. This analysis indicates patterns of interactions between the supervisor and the trainee.

NCS. Nonverbal Communication System (Tepper and Haase, 1978). This instrument can measure frequency of various nonverbal behaviors between counselor and client or between supervisor and trainee. It can also be modified and subjected to a sequential analysis similar to that described for the BIA.

Resource B

Trainee Information Form

The following form can be used to collect background information on trainees for use in practicum or internship. This information helps the supervisor to make an initial assessment of the developmental level of the trainee.

Trainee Background Information

Date _____

Name _____ Year entered program _____

Highest degree earned _____

Hours of individual counseling or psychotherapy experience
_____ Over how many years? _____

Hours of group counseling or psychotherapy experience _____
What types of groups? _____
_____

Hours of marriage and family counseling or psychotherapy experience _____ Over how many years? _____

Percentage of all counseling or psychotherapy experience that was supervised _____

Breadth of client populations served (please describe)

Professional environments you have worked in (for example, agencies). Please describe and note how long you were there and what your duties included.

Hours of direct supervision received (total)
   One-on-one _____
   Group or peer _____
Theoretical orientations to which you have been exposed

Preferred orientation

What assessment techniques or instruments have you used (administered, scored, and interpreted)? Please estimate how many of each.

Have you conducted intake assessments?   yes   no
Have you written psychological reports?   yes   no
   If so, how many and to whom (for example, physicians, courts, and so on)

Special experiences not covered above

What do you see as your professional strengths?

What do you see as your current professional weaknesses?

Other comments

Resource C

Guidelines for Conceptualizing a Case

The following form requires the trainee to integrate an array of information about a client. It is useful as a training device, as well as for providing the supervisor valuable information about both the trainee's conceptualization skills and client characteristics.

Case Conceptualization Format

1. *Identifying Data:* This section will include all relevant demographic information.

   1) age
   2) sex
   3) race
   4) marital status
   5) university classification
   6) living situation
   7) manner of dress
   8) physical appearance
   9) general self-presentation

2. *Presenting Problem:* This section should include a listing of the problem areas, from the client's perspective, noting par-

ticularly the client's view of their order of importance. Suggested items to focus upon:

1) Was there a precipitating set of circumstances?
2) How long has the problem(s) persisted?
3) Has this problem occurred before? What were the circumstances at the time?

3. *Relevant History:* This section will vary in comprehensiveness according to depth and length of treatment, and will vary in focus according to theoretical orientation and specific nature of the problem(s).

4. *Interpersonal Style:* This section should include a description of the client's orientation toward others in his environment and should include two sections:

   a) Is there an overall posture he/she takes toward others? What is the nature of his/her typical relationships? Karen Horney's conceptualization may be useful here:
      1) Moving toward (dependency, submission)
      2) Moving against (aggressive, dominance)
      3) Moving away (withdrawal)
      Is there a tendency toward one or the other polarity of dominance vs. submission, love vs. hate?

   b) How is the client's interpersonal stance manifested specifically within the therapeutic dyad? What is the client's interpersonal orientation toward the counselor?

5. *Environmental Factors:* This section should include:

   a) Elements in the environment which function as *stressors* to the client, both those centrally related to the problem and more peripheral stressors.

   b) Elements in the environment which function as *support* for the client; friends, family, living accommodations, recreational activities, financial situation.

6. *Personality Dynamics*

   A) *Cognitive Factors:* This section will include any data relevant to thinking and mental processes such as:
      a) intelligence
      b) mental alertness
      c) persistance of negative cognitions
      d) positive cognitions

      e)   nature and content of fantasy life

      f)   level of insight—client's "psychological minded-
ness" or ability to be aware and observant of
changes in feeling state and behavior and client's
ability to place his/her behavior in some interpre-
tive scheme and to consider hypotheses about his/
her own and others' behavior.

      g)   capacity for judgment. Client's ability to make de-
cisions and carry out the practical affairs of daily
living.

   B. *Emotional Factors*

      a)   typical or most common emotional states

      b)   mood during interview

      c)   appropriateness of affect

      d)   range of emotions the client has the capacity to
display

      e)   cyclical aspects of the client's emotional life

   C. *Behavioral Factors*

      a)   psychosomatic symptoms

      b)   other physical related symptoms

      c)   existence of persistent habits or mannerisms

      d)   sexual functioning

      e)   eating patterns

      f)   sleeping patterns

7. *Counselor's Conceptualization of the Problems:* This section will include a summary of the counselor's view of the
problem. Include only the most central and core dynamics
of the client's personality and note in particular the inter-
relationships between the major dynamics. What are the
common themes? What ties it all together? This is a synthe-
sis of all the above data and the essence of the conceptualization.

8. *Treatment Plan:* Based on the above information, describe
the plan you will follow to address the presenting and
emerging problems. Make it consistent with your theoretical orientation.

References

Alssid, L. L., and Hutchinson, W. R. "Comparison of Modeling Techniques in Counselor Training." *Counselor Education and Supervision,* 1977, *17,* 36–41.

American Personnel and Guidance Association. "Standards for the Preparation of Counselors and Other Personnel Services Specialists." *Personnel and Guidance Journal,* 1977, *55,* 596–601.

American Psychological Association. "Standards for Providers of Psychological Services." *American Psychologist,* 1977, *32,* 495–505.

American Psychological Association. *Criteria for Accreditation of Doctoral Training Programs and Internships in Professional Psychology.* Washington, D.C.: American Psychological Association, 1979.

American Psychological Association. "Ethical Principles of Psychologists." *American Psychologist,* 1981, *36,* 633–638.

Amidon, E. J. "A Technique for Analyzing Counselor-Counselee Interaction." In J. E. Adams (ed.), *Counseling and Guidance: A Summary View.* New York: Macmillan, 1965.

Anderson, R. P., and Anderson, G. V. "Development of an Instrument for Measuring Rapport." *Personnel and Guidance Journal,* 1962, *41,* 18–24.

197

Baltes, P. B. "Prototypical Paradigms and Questions in Life-Span Research on Development and Aging." *Gerontologist,* 1973, *13,* 458–467.

Baltes, P. B., Reese, H. W., and Nesselroade, J. R. *Life-Span Developmental Psychology: Introduction to Research Methods.* Belmont, Calif.: Wadsworth, 1977.

Barak, A., and LaCrosse, M. B. "Multi-Dimensional Perception of Counselor Behavior." *Journal of Counseling Psychology,* 1975, *22,* 471–476.

Barker, R. G., and Associates. *Habitats, Environments, and Human Behavior: Studies in Ecological Psychology and Eco-Behavioral Science.* San Francisco: Jossey-Bass, 1978.

Barrett-Lennard, G. T. *Relationship Inventory.* Armidale, Australia: University of New England, 1964.

Bartlett, W. E. "A Multidimensional Framework for the Analysis of Supervision of Counseling." *The Counseling Psychologist,* 1983, *11* (1), 9–17.

Bean, J. P., and Bradley, R. K. "Untangling the Satisfaction-Performance Relationship for College Students." Paper presented at the annual meeting of the American Educational Research Association, New Orleans, April 26, 1984.

Benack, S. "The Coding of Dimensions of Epistemological Thought in Young Men and Women." *Moral Education Forum,* 1982, *7* (2), 3–24.

Berg, K. S., and Stone, G. L. "Effects of Conceptual Level and Supervision Structure on Counselor Skill Development." *Journal of Counseling Psychology,* 1980, *27,* 500–509.

Bernard, J. M. "Supervisory Training: A Discrimination Model." *Counselor Education and Supervision,* 1979, *19,* 60–68.

Bernard, J. M. "Inservice Training for Clinical Supervisors." *Professional Psychology,* 1981, *12* (6), 740–748.

Bernstein, B. L., and Lecomte, C. "Supervisory-Type Feedback Effects: Feedback Discrepancy Level, Trainee Psychological Differentiation, and Immediate Responses." *Journal of Counseling Psychology,* 1979, *26,* 295–303.

Berzins, J. I., Bedner, R. L., and Severy, L. J. "The Problem of Intersource Consensus in Measuring Therapeutic Outcomes: New Data and Multivariate Perspectives." *Journal of Abnormal Psychology,* 1975, *84,* 10–19.

Blocher, D. H. *Developmental Counseling.* New York: Ronald Press, 1966.

Blocher, D. H. "Toward a Cognitive Developmental Approach to Counseling Supervision." *The Counseling Psychologist,* 1983, *11* (1), 27–34.

Blumberg, A. "Supervisor Behavior and Interpersonal Relations." *Educational Administration Quarterly,* 1968, *5,* 34–45.

Blumberg, A. "A System for Analyzing Supervisor-Teacher Interaction." In A. Simon and G. Boyer (eds.), *Mirrors for Behavior.* Vol. 3. Philadelphia: Research for Better Schools, 1970.

Bowman, J. T., and Roberts, G. T. "Effects of Tape-Recording and Supervisory Evaluation on Counselor Trainee Anxiety Levels." *Counselor Education and Supervision,* 1979, *19,* 20–26.

Boyd, J. *Counselor Supervision: Approaches, Preparation, Practices.* Muncie, Ind.: Accelerated Development, 1978.

Bratt, A., and Stoltenberg, C. D. "The Elaboration Likelihood Model and the Role of Affect." Unpublished manuscript, Texas Tech University, 1987.

Bruner, J. S. *Toward a Theory of Instruction.* New York: Norton, 1968.

Burkhart, R. B. "Training and Supervision of Crisis Workers." In A. K. Hess (ed.), *Psychotherapy Supervision: Theory, Research and Practice.* New York: Wiley, 1980.

Canon, H. J., and Brown, R. D. (eds.). *Applied Ethics in Student Services.* New Directions for Student Services, no. 30. San Francisco: Jossey-Bass, 1985.

Carkhuff, R. R. *Helping and Human Relations.* Vol. 2. New York: Holt, Rinehart & Winston, 1969.

Carkhuff, R. R., and Berenson, B. G. *Beyond Counseling and Psychotherapy.* New York: Holt, Rinehart & Winston, 1967.

Chickering, A. W. *Education and Identity.* San Francisco: Jossey-Bass, 1969.

Clark, B. R., and Trow, M. "The Organizational Context." In T. M. Newcomb and E. K. Wilson (eds.), *College Peer Groups: Problems and Prospects for Research.* Chicago: Aldine, 1966.

Cormier, S., and Bernard, J. M. "Ethical and Legal Responsibilities of Clinical Supervisors." *Personnel and Guidance Journal,* 1982, *60,* 486–491.

Cormier, L. S., Hackney, H., and Segrist, A. "Three Counselor Training Models: A Comparative Study." *Counselor Education and Supervision,* 1974, *14,* 95–104.

Dawidoff, D. J. *The Malpractice of Psychiatrists.* Springfield, Ill.: Thomas, 1973.

Dewey, J. *Experience and Education.* New York: Collier, 1963. (Originally published 1938.)

Dies, R. R. "Group Psychotherapy: Training and Supervision." In A. K. Hess (ed.), *Psych .therapy Supervision: Theory, Research and Practice.* New York: Wiley, 1980.

Division of Psychotherapy, American Psychological Association. "Recommended Standards for Psychotherapy Education in Psychology Doctoral Programs." *Professional Psychology,* 1971, *2,* 148–154.

Dixon, D. N., and Claiborn, C. D. "A Social Influence Approach to Counselor Supervision." In J. E. Maddux, C. D. Stoltenberg, and R. Rosenwein (eds.), *Social Processes in Clinical and Counseling Psychology.* New York: Springer-Verlag, 1987.

Duval, S., and Wicklund, R. A. *A Theory of Objective Self-Awareness.* Orlando, Fla.: Academic Press, 1972.

Egan, G. *The Skilled Helper: A Systematic Approach to Effective Helping.* (3rd ed.) Monterey, Calif.: Brooks/Cole, 1986.

Eiseley, L. *The Invisible Pyramid.* San Francisco: Jossey-Bass, 1970.

Ekstein, R., and Wallerstein, R. *The Teaching and Learning of Psychotherapy.* (2nd ed.) New York: International Universities Press, 1972.

Erikson, E. H. *Childhood and Society.* New York: Norton, 1963.

Erikson, E. H. *Identity, Youth, and Crisis.* New York: Norton, 1968.

Everett, C. A. "Supervision of Marriage and Family Therapy." In A. K. Hess (ed.), *Psychotherapy Supervision: Theory, Research and Practice.* New York: Wiley, 1980.

Flanders, N. A. *Interaction Analysis in the Classroom.* Minneapolis: University of Minnesota, 1960.

Flanders, N. A. "Interaction Analysis in the Classroom: A Manual for Observers." In A. Simon and G. Boyer (eds.), *Mirrors of Behavior*. Vol. 2. Philadelphia: Research for Better Schools, 1970.

Flavell, J. *Cognitive Development*. Englewood Cliffs, N.J.: Prentice-Hall, 1977.

Fleming, J. "The Role of Supervision in Psychiatric Training." *Bulletin of the Menninger Clinic*, 1953, *17*, 157–159.

Forsyth, D. R., and Ivey, A. E. "Microtraining: An Approach to Differential Supervision." In A. K. Hess (ed.), *Psychotherapy Supervision: Theory, Research and Practice*. New York: Wiley, 1980.

Fraleigh, P. W., and Buchheimer, A. "The Use of Peer Groups in Practicum Supervision." *Counselor Education and Supervision*, 1969, *8*, 284–288.

Friedlander, M. L., and Ward, L. G. "Development and Validation of the Supervisory Styles Inventory." *Journal of Counseling Psychology*, 1984, *31*, 541–557.

Gardner, H. *Developmental Psychology: An Introduction*. Boston: Little, Brown, 1978.

Gibbs, J. C. "Kohlberg's Stages of Moral Judgment: A Constructive Critique." *Harvard Educational Review*, 1977, *47*, 43–61.

Gilligan, C. *In a Different Voice: Psychological Theory and Women's Development*. Cambridge, Mass.: Harvard University Press, 1982.

Glenwick, D. S., and Stevens, E. "Vertical Supervision." In A. K. Hess (ed.), *Psychotherapy Supervision: Theory, Research and Practice*. New York: Wiley, 1980.

Goodyear, R. K., and Bradley, F. O. "Theories of Counselor Supervision: Points of Convergence and Divergence." *The Counseling Psychologist*, 1983, *11* (1), 59–67.

Gulanick, N., and Schmeck, R. R. "Modeling, Praise, and Criticism in Teaching Empathic Responding." *Counselor Education and Supervision*, 1977, *16*, 284–290.

Hackney, H., and Nye, L. S. *Counseling Strategies and Objectives*. Englewood Cliffs, N.J.: Prentice-Hall, 1973.

Hale, K. K., and Stoltenberg, C. D. "The Effects of Self-Awareness and Evaluation Apprehension on Counselor Trainee Anxiety." *The Clinical Supervisor*, forthcoming.

Handley, P. "Relationship Between Supervisors' and Trainees' Cognitive Styles and the Supervision Process." *Journal of Counseling Psychology*, 1982, *29*, 508-515.

Hart, G. M. *The Process of Clinical Supervision.* Baltimore, Md.: University Park Press, 1982.

Harvey, O. J., Hunt, D. E., and Schroder, H. M. *Conceptual Systems and Personality Organization.* New York: Wiley, 1961.

Heesacker, M. "Extrapolating From the Elaboration Likelihood Model of Attitude Change to Counseling." In F. J. Dorn (ed.), *The Social Influence Process in Counseling and Psychotherapy.* Springfield, Ill.: Thomas, 1986.

Heppner, P. P., and Handley, P. G. "A Study of the Interpersonal Influence Process in Supervision." *Journal of Counseling Psychology*, 1981, *28*, 437-444.

Heppner, P. P., and Roehlke, H. J. "Differences Among Supervisees at Different Levels of Training: Implications for a Developmental Model of Supervision." *Journal of Counseling Psychology*, 1984, *31*, 76-90.

Hess, A. K. (ed.). *Psychotherapy Supervision: Theory, Research and Practice.* New York: Wiley, 1980.

Hess, A. K., and Hess, K. A. "Psychotherapy Supervision: A Survey of Internship Training Practices." *Professional Psychology*, 1983, *14*, 504-513.

Hill, C., Carter, J., and O'Farrell, M. "A Case Study of the Process and Outcome of Time-Limited Counseling." *Journal of Counseling Psychology*, 1983, *30*, 3-18.

Hill, C. E., Charles, D., and Reed, K. G. "A Longitudinal Analysis of Changes in Counseling Skills During Doctoral Training in Counseling Psychology." *Journal of Counseling Psychology*, 1981, *28*, 428-436.

Hill, W. F. *Hill Interaction Matrix.* Los Angeles: Youth Study Center, University of Southern California, 1965.

Hoffman, M. L. "Empathy, Its Limitations, and Its Role in a Comprehensive Theory." In W. M. Kurtines and J. L. Gewirtz (eds.), *Morality, Moral Behavior, and Moral Development.* New York: Wiley, 1984.

Hogan, R. A. "Issues and Approaches in Supervision." *Psychotherapy: Theory, Research and Practice*, 1964, *1*, 139-141.

Hogan, R., and Busch, C. "Moral Action as Autointerpretation."
In W. M. Kurtines and J. L. Gewirtz (eds.), *Morality, Moral Behavior, and Moral Development.* New York: Wiley, 1984.

Holland, J. L. *The Psychology of Vocational Choice: A Theory of Personality Types and Model Environments.* Waltham, Mass.: Blaisdell, 1966.

Holloway, E. L. "The Interactional Structure of the Supervision Interview." *Journal of Counseling Psychology,* 1982, *29,* 309–317.

Holloway, E. L. "Outcome Evaluation in Supervision Research." *The Counseling Psychologist,* 1984, *12* (3), 167–174.

Holloway, E. L., and Johnson, R. "Group Supervision: Widely Practiced But Poorly Understood." *Counselor Education and Supervision,* 1985, *24,* 332–340.

Holloway, E. L., and Wampold, B. E. "Patterns of Verbal Behavior and Judgments of Satisfaction in the Supervision Interview." *Journal of Counseling Psychology,* 1983, *30,* 227–234.

Horan, J. J. "Behavioral Goals in Systematic Counselor Education." *Counselor Education and Supervision,* 1972, *11,* 286–291.

Hunt, D. E. *Matching Models in Education: The Coordination of Teaching Methods With Student Characteristics.* Toronto: Ontario Institute for Studies in Education, 1971.

Hunt, D. E. "Theorists Are Persons Too: On Preaching What You Practice." In C. A. Parker (ed.), *Encouraging Development in College Students.* Minneapolis: University of Minnesota Press, 1978.

Ivey, A. E. *Microcounseling: Innovations in Interviewing Training.* Springfield, Ill.: Thomas, 1971.

Ivey, A. E. *Developmental Therapy: Theory into Practice.* San Francisco: Jossey-Bass, 1986.

Ivey, A. E., and others. "Microcounseling and Attending Behavior: An Approach to Prepracticum Counselor Training." *Journal of Counseling Psychology,* 1968, *15,* part 2, 1–12.

Kagan, H. "Influencing Human Interaction—Eleven Years with IPR." *Canadian Counselor,* 1975, *9,* 74–97.

Kagan, N. "Influencing Human Interaction—Eighteen Years

with IPR." In A. K. Hess (ed.), *Psychotherapy Supervision: Theory, Research and Practice.* New York: Wiley, 1980.

Kagan, N., and Krathwohl, D. R. *Studies in Human Interaction: Interpersonal Process Recall Stimulated by Videotape.* East Lansing: Michigan State University, 1967.

Kell, B. L., and Burrow, J. M. *Developmental Counseling and Therapy.* Boston: Houghton Mifflin, 1970.

Kell, B. L., and Mueller, W. J. *Impact and Change: A Study of Counseling Relationships.* Englewood Cliffs, N.J.: Prentice-Hall, 1966.

Kiesler, D. J. "Some Myths of Psychotherapy Research and the Search for a Paradigm." *Psychological Bulletin,* 1966, *65,* 110-136.

Kohlberg, L. "Early Education: A Cognitive-Developmental View." *Child Development,* 1968, *39,* 1013-1062.

Krumboltz, J. D. "Behavioral Goals for Counseling." *Journal of Counseling Psychology,* 1966, *13,* 153-159.

Kuhn, D. "Development and Learning: European and American Traditions." *Contemporary Psychology,* 1975, *20,* 872-874.

Kuhn, D. "Introduction." In *Stage Theories of Cognitive and Moral Development.* Reprint no. 13. Cambridge, Mass.: Harvard Educational Review, 1978.

Kuhn, T. *The Structure of Scientific Revolutions.* Chicago: University of Chicago Press, 1962.

Lambert, M. F. "Supervisory and Counseling Process: A Comparative Study." *Counselor Education and Supervision,* 1974, *14,* 54-60.

Leddick, G. R., and Bernard, J. M. "The History of Supervision: A Critical Review." *Counselor Education and Supervision,* 1980, *19,* 186-196.

Levine, E. S., and Padilla, A. M. *Crossing Cultures in Therapy: Pluralistic Counseling for the Hispanic.* Monterey, Calif.: Brooks/Cole, 1980.

Lewin, K. *Principles of Topological Psychology.* New York: McGraw-Hill, 1936.

Lichtenberg, J. W., and Heck, E. J. "Analysis of Sequence and Pattern in Process Research." *Journal of Counseling Psychology,* 1986, *33,* 170-181.

Linden, J. D., Stone, S. L., and Shertzer, B. "Development and Evaluation of an Inventory for Rating Counseling." *Personnel and Guidance Journal,* 1965, *44,* 267–276.

Littrell, J. M., Lee-Borden, N., and Lorenz, J. A. "A Developmental Framework for Counseling Supervision." *Counselor Education and Supervision,* 1979, *19,* 129–136.

Loevinger, J. *Ego Development: Conceptions and Theories.* San Francisco: Jossey-Bass, 1976.

Loevinger, J. "Ego Maturity and Human Development." *Pupil Personnel Services Journal,* 1977, *6,* 19–24.

Loevinger, J., Wessler, R., and Redmore, C. *Measuring Ego Development.* 2 vols. San Francisco: Jossey-Bass, 1970.

Loganbill, C., and Hardy, E. "In Defense of Eclecticism." *The Counseling Psychologist,* 1983, *11* (1), 79.

Loganbill, C., Hardy, E., and Delworth, U. "Supervision: A Conceptual Model." *The Counseling Psychologist,* 1982, *10* (1), 3–42.

Loganbill, C., and Stoltenberg, C. D. "A Case Conceptualization Format: A Training Device for Practicum." *Counselor Education and Supervision,* 1983, *22,* 235–241.

Looft, W. R. "Socialization and Personality Throughout the Life Span: An Examination of Contemporary Psychological Approaches." In P. B. Baltes and K. W. Schaie (eds.), *Life-Span Developmental Psychology: Personality and Socialization.* Orlando, Fla.: Academic Press, 1973.

McCarthy, P. R., Danish, S. J., and D'Augelli, A. R. "A Follow-Up Evaluation of Helping Skills Training." *Counselor Education and Supervision,* 1977, *17,* 29–35.

McNeill, B. W., Stoltenberg, C. D., and Pierce, R. A. "Supervisees' Perceptions of Their Development: A Test of the Counselor Complexity Model." *Journal of Counseling Psychology,* 1985, *32,* 630–633.

Mahler, M. S. "Separation-Individuation." *The Selected Papers of Margaret S. Mahler, M.D.* Vol. 2. New York: Jason Aronson, 1979.

Mahon, B. R., and Altmann, H. A. "Skill Training: Cautions and Recommendations." *Counselor Education and Supervision,* 1977, *17,* 42–50.

Marecek, J., and Johnson, M. "Gender and the Process of Therapy." In A. M. Brodsky and R. T. Hare-Mustin (eds.), *Women and Psychotherapy: An Assessment of Research and Practice.* New York: Guilford, 1980.

Maslach, C. "Job Burnout: How People Cope." *Public Welfare,* 1978, *36,* 56–58.

Miars, R. D., and others. "Variation in Supervision Process Across Trainee Experience Levels." *Journal of Counseling Psychology,* 1983, *30,* 403–412.

Michaels, L. F. "The Development of an Anchored Rating Scale for Evaluating Psychotherapy Skills." Unpublished doctoral dissertation, Colorado State University, 1982.

Miller, G. D. "Developmental Theory: High Promise for Guidance Practice." *Pupil Personnel Services Journal,* 1977, *6,* 1–17.

Newcomb, T. M., Joenig, K. E., Flacks, R., and Warwick, D. P. *Persistence and Change: Bennington College and Its Students After 25 Years.* New York: Wiley, 1967.

Newman, A. S. "Ethical Issues in the Supervision of Psychotherapy." *Professional Psychology,* 1981, *12,* 690–695.

Orton, J. W. "Areas of Focus in Supervising Counseling Practicum Students in Groups." *Personnel and Guidance Journal,* 1965, *44,* 167–170.

Payne, P. A., and Gralinski, D. M. "Effects of Supervisor Style and Empathy on Counselor Learning." *Journal of Counseling Psychology,* 1968, *15,* 517–521.

Payne, P. A., Weiss, S. D., and Kapp, R. A. "Didactic, Experiential, and Modeling Factors in the Learning of Empathy." *Journal of Counseling Psychology,* 1972, *19,* 425–429.

Payne, P. A., Winter, D. E., and Bell, G. E. "Effects of Supervision Style on the Learning of Empathy in a Supervision Analogue." *Counselor Education and Supervision,* 1972, *23,* 212–215.

Payton, C. R. "Addressing the Special Needs of Minority Women." In N. J. Evans (ed.), *Facilitating the Development of Women.* New Directions for Student Services, no. 29. San Francisco: Jossey-Bass, 1985.

Peabody, S. A., and Gelso, C. J. "Countertransference and Empathy: The Complex Relationship Between Two Divergent Concepts in Counseling." *Journal of Counseling Psychology,* 1982, *29,* 240-245.

Perry, W. G., Jr. *Forms of Intellectual and Ethical Development in the College Years.* New York: Holt, Rinehart & Winston, 1968.

Perry, W. G., Jr. "Intellectual and Ethical Forms of Development." *Pupil Personnel Services Journal,* 1977, *6,* 61-68.

Pervin, L. A. "Performance and Satisfaction as a Function of Individual-Environment Fit." *Psychological Bulletin,* 1968, *69,* 56-68.

Petty, R. E., and Cacioppo, J. T. *Attitude and Persuasion: Classic and Contemporary Approaches.* Dubuque, Iowa: Brown, 1981.

Phillips, D. C., and Kelly, M. E. "Hierarchical Theories of Development in Education and Psychology." *Harvard Educational Review,* 1975, *45,* 351-375.

Piaget, J. *The Child's Conception of the World.* Orlando, Fla.: Harcourt Brace Jovanovich, 1929.

Piaget, J. *Structuralism.* New York: Basic Books, 1970.

Piaget, J. *Biology and Knowledge: An Essay on the Relations Between Organic Regulations and Cognitive Processes.* Chicago: University of Chicago Press, 1971.

Pierce, R. M., Carkhuff, R. R., and Berenson, B. G. "The Effects of High and Low Functioning Counselors Upon Counselors in Training." *Journal of Clinical Psychology,* 1967, *23,* 212-215.

Pierce, R. M., and Schauble, P. G. "Graduate Training of Facilitative Counselors: The Effects of Individual Supervision." *Journal of Counseling Psychology,* 1970, *17,* 210-215.

Pierce, R. M., and Schauble, P. G. "Follow-up Study on the Effects of Individual Supervision in Graduate School Training." *Journal of Counseling Psychology,* 1971, *18,* 186-187.

Pope, K. S., Levenson, H., and Schover, L. R. "Sexual Intimacy in Psychology Training: Results and Implications of a National Survey." *American Psychologist,* 1979, *34,* 682-689.

Pope, K. S., Schover, L. R., and Levenson, H. "Sexual Behavior Between Clinical Supervisors and Trainees: Implications for

Professional Standards." *Professional Psychology,* 1980, *10,* 157–162.

Rabinowitz, F. E., Heppner, P. P., and Roehlke, H. J. "Descriptive Study of Process and Outcome Variables of Supervision Over Time." *Journal of Counseling Psychology,* 1985, *33,* 292–300.

Ralph, N. B. "Learning Psychotherapy: A Developmental Perspective." *Psychiatry,* 1980, *43,* 243–250.

Raphael, R. D. "Supervisee Experience: The Effect on Supervisor Verbal Responses." Paper presented at the annual meeting of the American Psychological Association, Washington, D.C., August 1982.

Reising, G. N., and Daniels, M. H. "A Study of Hogan's Model of Counselor Development and Supervision." *Journal of Counseling Psychology,* 1983, *30,* 235–244.

Rest, J. "Comprehension Preference and Spontaneous Usage in Moral Judgment." In L. Kohlberg and E. Turiel (eds.), *Recent Research in Moral Development.* New York: Holt, Rinehart & Winston, 1973.

Riegel, K. F. "The Dialectics of Human Development." *American Psychologist,* 1976, *31,* 689–700.

Rioch, M. J., Coulter, W. R., and Weinberger, D. M. *Dialogue for Therapists: Dynamics of Learning and Supervision.* San Francisco: Jossey-Bass, 1976.

Rogers, C. R. "The Necessary and Sufficient Conditions of Therapeutic Personality Change." *Journal of Counseling Psychology,* 1957, *21,* 95–103.

Rosenberg, M. J. "The Conditions and Consequences of Evaluation Apprehension." In R. Rosenthal and R. L. Rosnow (eds.), *Artifact in Behavioral Research.* Orlando, Fla.: Academic Press, 1969.

Russell, R. K., Crimmings, A. M., and Lent, R. W. "Counselor Training and Supervision: Theory and Research." In S. D. Brown and R. W. Lent (eds.), *Handbook of Counseling Psychology.* New York: Wiley, 1984.

Salkind, N. J. *Theories of Human Development.* (2nd ed.) New York: Wiley, 1985.

Sansbury, D. L. "Developmental Supervision From a Skills Perspective." *The Counseling Psychologist,* 1982, *10* (1), 53-57.

Sarason, S. B. *The Creation of Settings and the Future Societies.* San Francisco: Jossey-Bass, 1972.

Schmidt, L. D., and Meara, N. M. "Ethical, Professional, and Legal Issues in Counseling Psychology." In S. D. Brown and R. W. Lent (eds.), *Handbook of Counseling Psychology.* New York: Wiley, 1984.

Selfridge, F. F., and others. "Sensitivity-Oriented Versus Didactically-Oriented Inservice Counselor Training." *Journal of Counseling Psychology,* 1975, *22,* 156-159.

Sidman, M. *Tactics of Scientific Research.* New York: Basic Books, 1960.

Slovenko, R. "Legal Issues in Psychotherapy Supervision." In A. K. Hess (ed.), *Psychotherapy Supervision: Theory, Research and Practice.* New York: Wiley, 1980.

Smith, M. J. "Ethnic Minorities: Life Stress, Social Support, and Mental Health Issues." *The Counseling Psychologist,* 1985, *13* (4), 537-579.

Spooner, S. E., and Stone, S. C. "Maintenance of Specific Counseling Skills Over Time." *Journal of Counseling Psychology,* 1977, *24,* 66-71.

Stoltenberg, C. D. "Approaching Supervision From a Developmental Perspective: The Counselor Complexity Model." *Journal of Counseling Psycnology,* 1981, *28,* 59-65.

Stoltenberg, C. D. "Elaboration Likelihood and the Counseling Process." In F. J. Dorn (ed.), *The Social Influence Process in Counseling and Psychotherapy.* Springfield, Ill.: Thomas, 1986.

Stoltenberg, C. D., and McNeill, B. W. "Attitude Change in Counseling and Psychotherapy: The Elaboration Likelihood Model." In J. E. Maddux, C. D. Stoltenberg, and R. Rosenwein (eds.), *Social Processes in Clinical and Counseling Psychology.* New York: Springer-Verlag, 1987.

Stoltenberg, C. D., Pierce, R. A., and McNeill, B. W. "Effects of Experience on Counselor Needs." *The Clinical Supervisor,* 1987, *5,* 23-32.

Stoltenberg, C. D., Solomon, G. S., and Ogden, L. "Comparing

Supervisee and Supervisor Initial Perceptions of Supervision: Do They Agree?" *The Clinical Supervisor,* 1986, *4,* 53–61.

Stone, G. L. "Effects of Experiences on Supervisor Planning." *Journal of Counseling Psychology,* 1980, *27,* 84–88.

Strong, S. R. "Counseling: An Interpersonal Influence Process." *Journal of Counseling Psychology,* 1968, *15,* 215–224.

Sue, D. W. *Counseling the Culturally Different.* New York: Wiley, 1981.

Sue, D. W., and others. "Position Paper: Cross-Cultural Counseling Competencies." *The Counseling Psychologist,* 1982, *10* (2), 45–52.

Task Force on Sex Bias and Sex Role Stereotyping in Psychotherapeutic Practice. "Guidelines for Therapy with Women." *American Psychologist,* 1978, *33* (12), 1122–1123.

Tepper, D. T., and Haase, R. D. "Verbal and Nonverbal Communication of Facilitative Conditions." *Journal of Counseling Psychology,* 1978, *25,* 35–44.

Tinsley, H. E. A., and Tinsley, D. J. "Different Needs, Interests, and Abilities of Effective and Ineffective Counselor Trainees: Implications for Counselor Selection." *Journal of Counseling Psychology,* 1977a, *24,* 83–86.

Tinsley, H. E. A., and Tinsley, D. J. "Relationship Between Scores on the Omnibus Personality Inventory and Counselor Trainee Effectiveness." *Journal of Counseling Psychology,* 1977b, *24,* 522–526.

Truax, C. B., and Carkhuff, R. R. *Toward Effective Counseling and Psychotherapy: Training and Practice.* Chicago: Aldine, 1967.

Tyler, L. E. *Individuality: Human Possibilities and Personal Choice in the Psychological Development of Men and Women.* San Francisco: Jossey-Bass, 1978.

Van Hoose, W. H., and Kottler, J. A. *Ethical and Legal Issues in Counseling and Psychotherapy.* 2nd ed. San Francisco: Jossey-Bass, 1985.

Vasquez, M. J., and McKinley, D. "A Conceptual Model—Reactions and an Extension." *The Counseling Psychologist,* 1982, *10* (1), 59–63.

Wampold, B. E. "State of the Art in Sequential Analysis: Comment on Lichtenberg and Heck." *Journal of Counseling Psychology*, 1986, *33*, 182–185.

Wasik, B. H., and Fishbein, J. E. "Problem Solving: A Model for Supervision in Professional Psychology." *Professional Psychology*, 1982, *13* (4), 559–564.

Werner, H. "The Concept of Development From a Comparative and Organismic Point of View." In D. Harris (ed.), *The Concept of Development*. Minneapolis: University of Minnesota Press, 1957.

Whitehead, A. N. "Permanence and Flux." In J. H. Randall, Jr., J. Buchler, and E. U. Shirk (eds.), *Readings in Philosophy*. (2nd ed.) New York: Barnes and Noble, 1950.

Whiteley, J. M. (ed.). "Supervision in Counseling I." *Counseling Psychologist*, 1982, *10* (1), 1–96.

Whiteley, J. M. (ed.). "Supervision in Counseling II." *Counseling Psychologist*, 1983, *11* (1), 1–112.

Wicker, A. W. *An Introduction to Ecological Psychology*. Monterey, Calif.: Brooks/Cole, 1979.

Wiley, M. O'L. *Developmental Counseling Supervision: Person-Environment Congruency, Satisfaction, and Learning*. Paper presented at the annual meeting of the American Psychological Association, Washington, D.C., August 1982.

Worthington, E. L., Jr. "An Empirical Investigation of Supervision of Counselors as They Gain Experience." *Journal of Counseling Psychology*, 1984, *31*, 63–75.

Worthington, E. L., Jr. "Changes in Supervision as Counselors and Supervisors Gain Experience: A Review." *Professional Psychology*, 1987.

Worthington, E. L., Jr., and Roehlke, H. J. "Effective Supervision as Perceived by Beginning Counselors-in-Training." *Journal of Counseling Psychology*, 1979, *26*, 64–73.

Worthington, E. L., Jr., and Stern, A. "Effects of Supervisor and Supervisee Degree Level and Gender on the Supervisory Relationship." *Journal of Counseling Psychology*, 1985, *32* (2), 252–262.

Yogev, S. "An Eclectic Model of Supervision: A Developmental

Sequence for Beginning Psychotherapy Students." *Profes-sional Psychology*, 1982, *13*, 236-243.

Zucker, P. J., and Worthington, E. L., Jr. "Supervision of In-terns and Post-Doctoral Applicants for Licensure in Univer-sity Counseling Centers." *Journal of Counseling Psychology*, 1986, *33*, 87-89.

Index

A

Accommodation, 37, 46, 52, 78, 86, 105
Accountability, 173-174
Affect, 109
Affective interventions, 68-69
Age: developmental stage and, 9; of trainee, 19, 47
Altmann, H. A., 16
Ambiguity, Level 1 trainees and, 63-64
Ambivalence, of Level 2 trainees, 69, 70, 82, 90
American College Personnel Association (ACPA), 100, 169-170
American Psychological Association (APA), 100, 152, 163, 169, 170, 171, 172, 178-179
Amidon, E. J., 115
Anderson, R. P., 188
Anxiety: of Level 1 trainees, 41, 53, 55, 56, 60, 61-62, 65, 87
Assessment instruments, 123-125, 183-189
Assessment of developmental level, 111-136; behavioral observations, 115-117; broad-based, 121; cli-ent ratings, 119; current procedures, 113-121; fundamentals of, 121-123; initial, typical, 112; instruments for, 123-124, 183-189; of intervention skills competence, 129-133; need for, 111-113; ongoing, 122; qualitative, within domains, 127, 128-133, 135-136; supervisee measures, 117-119; supervisor measures, 113-115, 124-127; of supervisors, 158-160; theoretical orientation and, 113-114; trainee understanding of need for, 122-123; work samples in, 119-120
Assessment techniques, of trainees, 36; at Level 1, 55; at Level 2, 76; at Level 3, 97. *See also* Interpersonal assessment
Assimilation, 37, 46, 52, 77, 85-86
Attitude change, 87-88; Elaboration Likelihood Model of, 45-46
Audiotaping, 61, 66
Autonomy of trainees, 32, 36; assessment of, 132-133; of Level 2 trainees, 72; of Level 3 supervisors, 157; of Level 3 trainees, 40, 44, 94-95, 106. *See also* Depen-

213